GOLF'S DREAM 18s

GOLF'S DREAM 18s

FANTASY COURSES COMPRISED
OF OVER 300 HOLES
FROM AROUND THE WORLD

DAVID BARRETT

PHOTOGRAPHY BY

L. C. LAMBRECHT

RUSSELL KIRK

EVAN SCHILLER

DAVID SCALETTI

JOHN AND JEANNINE HENEBRY

AND OTHERS

ABRAMS, NEW YORK

CONTENTS

INTRODUCTION

There are probably a couple of hundred truly great golf courses around the world. But there are thousands of great golf holes located on those great courses and on countless very good layouts.

Those great holes are well scattered geographically, of course, but what if they were gathered into groups of eighteen to make mythical courses? That's what I set out to do with *Golf's Dream 18s.*

When architects design a golf course, they work with the land given to them, though these days, when extensive earthmoving is possible, they are also free to use their imaginations. In designing these Dream 18s (there are eighteen of them in all), I used fully formed holes as my building blocks for mythical layouts.

I was free from worry about actual terrain or routing. But the Dream 18s are designed to play (if only in your head) like real courses, with total par ranging from 70 to 73.

These 18s have themes, such as Scenic Holes, Historic Holes, Exclusive Holes, etc. In most cases, there is variety in the lengths and difficulties of holes, types of shots called for, placement of hazards, etc. The exceptions are 18s such

as Long Holes (the course comes to a total of 8,748 yards!), Short Holes (total 5,011 yards—all world-class holes), Hard Holes, and the like. Even in these instances, I strove for variety in other aspects.

We have made up a scorecard for each Dream 18, showing the yardage from five sets of tees. Not all of the holes selected have that many tee markers, of course, so the numbers have been filled in by making a judgment on which existing tee is most appropriate. The black tees are considered to be for male pros and scratch players, the blue tees for male low handicappers, the white tees for average male players or female pros, the gold tees for male seniors or low-handicap women, and the red tees for average women or juniors.

While many books about golf courses and holes focus on how the holes play from the championship tees for the best players, I have made an effort to give consideration to all levels of players in the selection of the holes and also in the descriptions.

It's all wrapped up at the end with the Ultimate Dream 18, taking the best holes from the other seventeen lists.

The Ultimate 18 was the only one where I used a strict correspondence of hole numbers, with the 1st hole being an actual 1st hole, on down the line to the 18th hole being an actual 18th hole.

None of these Dream 18s can be said to represent the definitive list of the eighteen greatest holes in its respective category. That's partly because there is no such thing; judging golf holes is too subjective. It's also because many great holes were candidates in more than one category, but each hole was allowed to appear only once (except for a second appearance in the Ultimate Dream 18). Some other rules: The maximum number of holes for any course was four and no course could contribute more than one hole to any given Dream 18. All geographic areas of the world, all eras of golf architecture, and a wide variety of golf course designers are represented.

In putting this book together, my thanks go to editor Margaret L. Kaplan and managing editor Andrea Colvin at Harry N. Abrams, designer Jessica Shatan Heslin for making it look so good, and to Laurie Platt Winfrey and Cristian Peña at Carousel Research for gathering all of the photographs. Those photos came from a variety of sources, but we leaned most heavily on the excellent work of photographers Larry Lambrecht, David Scaletti, Russell Kirk, and Evan Schiller.

At home, thanks go to my wife, Ludmila, and children, Michael and Sophia, for their support and understanding.

The hardest part of this book was probably making the selections, which was akin to solving a giant jigsaw puzzle. In the end, it all fit together, and I had fun doing it.

I hope you enjoy "playing" these courses, too, or at least dreaming about them. —*David Barrett*

SCENIC

HOLES

One of golf's greatest attributes is that it is played on expansive pieces of open ground, very often in beautiful settings. Our impressions and memories of a golf course are formed not only by the layout itself, but by the scenery that we view as we make our way around. The 18th hole at Pebble Beach, for example, is a very good hole, but it becomes a great one when you consider its magnificent setting along the Pacific Ocean.

There's something about playing alongside an ocean that is particularly invigorating for a golfer, all the more so if a portion of the water or beach must be carried with a shot. The sound of crashing surf and the blue vistas stretching to the horizon never fail to inspire. That type of hole is well represented on our list.

Mountain views also register highly. There is a separate Dream 18 on Mountain Holes, and any of those selections could have been candidates for this list; we have chosen two particularly stunning mountain settings for the Scenic category. When it comes to rugged beauty, a desert landscape replete with cacti fills the bill, so a couple of desert holes are included.

Some superbly scenic holes don't appear here, but have been slotted in other categories. They include the 16th at Cypress Point and the 6th at New South Wales (both in Strategic Holes), the 8th at Pebble Beach (Holes Anyone Can Play), and the 9th at Royal County Down (Long Holes). But Cypress Point and Pebble Beach do have holes on the Scenic list. Indeed, the 17th and 18th holes, respectively, on those two courses that are just a few miles apart on California's Monterey Peninsula, occupy the same positions on this Dream 18.

The Scenic 18 plays to a par of 70 because there are six par 3s—there were just too many par-3 candidates to limit it to four of them. It's a fairly short course (the white tees barely crack 6,000 yards), but, trust us, it's no pushover. It's going to be hard to get around without putting a couple of balls in the water, and if you start bailing out to the other side it will be hard to make pars. Not to mention the difficulty of keeping your mind on the game surrounded by all that luscious scenery.

Left: **No. 9 The Challenge at Manele, Lanai City, Hawaii** ↻ 12th Hole, 202 Yards, Par 3 *See page 17 for description.*

		Par	Black	Blue	White	Gold	Red			Par	Black	Blue	White	Gold	Red
1	Desert Highlands 1	4	356	339	313	285	212	10	Sebonack 18	5	560	525	501	501	428
2	Pelican Hill (North) 17	5	558	540	525	483	382	11	Vintage (Mountain) 16	4	409	387	370	314	310
3	Old Head 4	4	427	423	415	388	357	12	Nirwana Bali 7	3	214	194	194	144	130
4	Banff Springs 4	3	171	157	157	157	78	13	Pacific Dunes 13	4	444	390	390	371	336
5	Liberty National 17	4	445	428	387	348	297	14	Kauri Cliffs 7	3	221	200	176	149	106
6	Kawana (Fuji) 15	5	475	470	470	415	385	15	Pinnacle Point 8	4	350	326	310	300	273
7	Casa de Campo (Teeth of the Dog) 7	3	229	224	188	168	91	16	Greywolf 6	3	200	175	155	142	77
								17	Cypress Point 17	4	393	382	382	382	355
8	Cabo del Sol (Ocean) 18	4	430	419	385	358	275	18	Pebble Beach 18	5	543	543	532	509	455
9	Challenge at Manele 12	3	202	185	153	103	65	**In**		35	3334	3122	3010	2812	2470
Out		35	3293	3185	2993	2705	2142	**TOTAL**		70	6627	6307	6003	5517	4612

No. 1 Desert Highlands, Scottsdale, Arizona

○

1st Hole, 356 Yards, Par 4

There's no water in sight, but the desert can be beautiful, too. The amazing thing is how natural this hole feels—if you ignore the fact that in its natural state you wouldn't be looking down at lush green grass from the elevated tee.

It's the areas surrounding the fairway that remind you where you are. The tee is on a ledge some 125 feet above the landing area, making the landscape of boulders and cactus that lies between the tee and fairway less intimidating. To the right of the fairway, more desert flora and sand extend

to a tower of rock to the right of the green. The left side is a bit more open, but hit it far enough in that direction and you'll find the desert, too.

A couple of bunkers pinch the fairway, which means the prudent play on this Jack Nicklaus–designed hole is to lay up with an iron or fairway wood off the tee for accuracy. However, with the distance gains brought about by today's equipment, it is now possible for some players to think about driving the green (something that wasn't possible back in 1983 when Desert Highlands hosted the first Skins Game). It's a risky move. Misfire and you may be picking cactus spikes out of your backside after your second shot.

No. 2 Pelican Hill Golf Club
(Ocean North Course),
Newport Coast, California

⌒

17th Hole, 558 Yards, Par 5

Designer Tom Fazio says that at the two courses at Pelican Hill "you have this 'wow' factor that goes on and on, hole after hole." The most awestruck "wows" are heard on this beauty. It plays toward the ocean, making for a blue backdrop that extends to the horizon, with a lone tree next to the green adding just the right touch to make this a postcard hole.

There is water to the right, as well, in the form of an ocean inlet. To the right of the green is a deep bunker and then a drop-off. That drop-off extends diagonally back down the hole, cutting into the landing area for the second shot. The safe play for the average player is toward the left, but that makes for a longer third. If the longer hitter can carry the right-hand fairway bunkers and avoid the hazard, he will be rewarded with a relatively simple pitch from short of the green, even if he doesn't get home in two.

The layout originally opened in 1993, and was closed from 2005 to 2007 for renovation while a resort hotel was being developed. The resort is now open, but both courses are still available to daily-fee play.

No. 3 Old Head Golf Links, Kinsale, Ireland

4th Hole, 427 Yards, Par 4

There's no other golf parcel in the world quite like the one on which Old Head was built in southwest Ireland. It's a 220-acre diamond-shaped promontory, jutting into the sea so that it's almost an island. The land sits as much as 300 feet above the sea, framed by rocky cliffs.

The size of the promontory happens to be perfect for a golf course, but it was being used for farming until brothers John and Patrick O'Connor bought it in 1989. The course, with a design team led by American Ron Kirby, opened in 1997, featuring nine holes that play along the cliffs.

One of those is the 4th, named the Razor's Edge, which doglegs to the left around an inlet. The right side is the safe side on the tee shot, especially as it is sloped toward the center of the fairway. Long hitters have a choice of carrying a fairway bunker to cut the dogleg or laying up to the right of it.

The reason for taking the gamble is to shorten a demanding second shot to a narrow, elevated green that is nearly at the tip of the promontory. There are no bunkers around the putting surface, but not much grass around it either. To the left and rear is a hazard in the form of cliffs. To the right is a rock outcropping. The only place to miss without a disaster is short of the green. The ball may roll back down a slope, but at least it will be playable.

No. 4 Fairmont Banff Springs Golf Course, Banff, Alberta, Canada

4th Hole, 171 Yards, Par 3

Carries over water hazards were not commonplace in golf architecture of the 1920s. But when an avalanche during the winter of 1927 led to the formation of a small lake on the property where the Banff Springs Golf Course was about to be built, designer Stanley Thompson could not resist. He modified his plans and designed what is now the 4th hole of the Banff Springs layout.

The hole drops seventy feet from tee to green, making the carry less frightening even to golfers of the 1920s when steel shafts were still just a novelty. The water doesn't extend all the way to the green, but a slope in front means that a ball coming up short may roll back into the hazard. Low-handicappers won't be too worried about the water, unless they take too big a risk going for a front pin. The green has a significant back-to-front slope and also tends to gather shots from the sides toward the middle—not necessarily a good thing when you're trying to get your tee shot close to the hole.

The beauty of the hole comes from the combination of the lake, the six bunkers ringing the green, the tall timber behind the putting surface, and, most dramatically, the rocky peak looming just behind the trees. The hole is called the Devil's Cauldron, but in truth it seems more like heaven for a golfer.

No. 5 Liberty National Golf Club, Jersey City, New Jersey

↻

17th Hole, 445 Yards, Par 4

There's no other course with a setting like Liberty National. Less than 1,000 feet away from the site of the clubhouse, the Statue of Liberty rises out of New York Harbor. There are inspiring views of the statue and its upraised torch from many points on the course; one of the best is from the 17th fairway, from which point the pedestal cannot be seen and it looks as if Lady Liberty is walking in the rough. The Manhattan skyline is another impressive sight from the Liberty National grounds.

This beautiful spot arose, ironically, from an industrial wasteland. The 160-acre parcel was purchased by former Reebok CEO Paul Fireman in 1998, and it took eight years, $130 million, and two million cubic feet of soil to turn a former brownfield into a high-priced golf club. The course is already scheduled to host a PGA Tour event, the Barclays, in 2009.

The Bob Cupp/Tom Kite design is rated as among the most difficult in the New York metro area, a region known for tough courses. The 17th hole fits right in as it turns the screws on players approaching the finish. The fairway snakes back and forth, dotted with bunkers along the way, with tall fescue lining both sides of the fairway to give a Scottish feel to a hole that is overlooked by one of America's icons.

No. 6 Kawana Resort (Fuji Course), Ito, Japan

୨

15th Hole, 475 Yards, Par 5

Kawana can rightfully be called the Pebble Beach of Japan, as it features a luxury hotel and a world-class golf course that hugs the Pacific Ocean. There are actually two courses at Kawana, but the one of note is the Fuji Course, designed by Englishman Charles Alison and opened in 1936. Of the site, Alison said, "The scenery resembles that of the French Riviera, but at not a single spot between the Italian and Spanish frontiers can be found so superb a combination of sea, cliffs, trees, and mountains."

Mount Fuji can be seen in the distance on a clear day, but the 15th hole has plenty of visual appeal in its own right. It's a parkland setting that happens to border the ocean, with lush vegetation marking the line between the land and the top of the cliffs that drop down to an ocean inlet. The drive from the very elevated back tee must carry the inlet.

Taking a line farther to the left from the back tee will cut off more distance, but there are two reasons not to go too far in that direction. A big hook will be lost in the hazard, but also a drive in the left side of the fairway will be blocked from going for the green in two as the putting surface is tucked behind a row of trees at the top of the cliff. It is these trees that make the hole a legitimate par 5 despite its relatively skimpy yardage. Also noteworthy is the roller-coaster fairway, which can provide a difficult downhill lie for the second shot.

**No. 7 Casa de Campo (Teeth of the Dog Course),
La Romana, Dominican Republic**

ↄ

7th Hole, 229 Yards, Par 3

**No. 8 Cabo del Sol (Ocean Course),
Cabo San Lucas, Mexico**

ↄ

18th Hole, 430 Yards, Par 4

This is one of seven holes that skirt the ocean on this Pete Dye layout that opened in 1971 and has reigned ever since as the best course in the Caribbean. It's a long par 3 that plays over a small inlet, with the ocean to the left, but the good news is that there is some margin for error both short and left. The bad news is that a miss in either spot will probably end up in a deep waste bunker that wraps around the green. And with the carry being slightly longer to the left, it's still better to favor the right side, especially with a long iron or fairway wood in your hands.

A par 3 of 229 yards from the tips (or 188 yards from the middle tee for the average player) is never easy. But the architect has given you enough margin for error to let you relax at least a little bit and take in the view, which includes not only the water extending to the horizon, but also tropical trees lining the right side and back of the green.

Designer Jack Nicklaus used Cabo del Sol's distinctive desert-meets-ocean setting to maximum effect on the 18th hole. The view that faces the golfer from the tee is rugged and beautiful at the same time, with cactus, boulders, and scrub bush directly ahead and the pure blue Pacific to the right. The hole bends to the right, with the green visible in the distance beyond a section of sandy beach. Completing the picture is the striking Spanish architecture of the clubhouse and resort behind the green.

The tee shot requires a carry—quite manageable—over a wasteland to a wide portion of the fairway. Then the beach/desert cuts into the fairway, gradually narrowing it until it is practically a sliver. Again, it's not a huge carry for the second shot, with the fairway widening well short of the green. It's not an especially long hole, and big hitters might have to lay up off the tee to avail themselves of the generous part of the landing area. The trouble is plainly visible (there's desert to the left of the fairway, too), but there is plenty of room to play, and there are always the soothing sights and sounds of the ocean.

No. 9 The Challenge at Manele, Lanai City, Hawaii

12th Hole, 202 Yards, Par 3

The challenge at *this* hole at Manele is to keep your mind on the shot at hand. That's hard to do when staring you in the face is a sheer 200-foot cliff, with surf crashing far below and a green perched perilously on the other side. The cliff hugs the left side of the green just as tightly, so you know what you need to do: make sure you don't miss short or left. That's after you put away your camera, of course.

It's all carry from the back two sets of tees, but mid- to high-handicappers or the faint of heart can move to the next tee box at 153 yards, which is set more to the right so the chasm need not be carried. Anything to the left, though, is still wet—after its long trip down to the ocean.

By the way, the tee on this Jack Nicklaus–designed resort course is a picture-perfect spot for more than just golfers. It also served as the site of the wedding of Bill and Melinda Gates in 1994.

See page 8 for photo.

No. 10 Sebonack Golf Club, Southampton, New York

18th Hole, 560 Yards, Par 5

What could possibly have brought headstrong course designers Jack Nicklaus and Tom Doak together to collaborate on a layout? Perhaps only the opportunity to design a course on the same sandy soil as neighboring National Golf Links and Shinnecock Hills, spiced with the prospect of fashioning a couple of holes right along Great Peconic Bay.

They got together and came up with a winner, especially at the par-5 18th hole, which combines beauty with sound design. From the elevated tee, the golfer can gaze down the length of the hole, with the fairway separated from the beach and water on the left by a row of trees. A large cross bunker looms in the fairway, but it can be carried with the second shot after a decent drive. The key strategic element is that a drive favoring the left side—closer to the trouble—makes for an easier second shot, whether it's a layup or a go at the wicked two-tier green.

Owner Michael Pascucci deserves credit on two fronts. First, for having the idea to bring Nicklaus and Doak together. Second, for convincing them to make the 18th a par 5 instead of the par 4 they wanted. It was the only design decision they let him make, but it was a good one.

No. 11 The Vintage Club (Mountain Course), Indian Wells, California
↻
16th Hole, 409 Yards, Par 4

Golf great Walter Hagen once advised, "You're only here for a short visit. Be sure to stop and smell the flowers along the way." That's certainly possible at the Mountain Course's 16th hole, where the tee boxes and the water hazard between the tee and fairway are lined with beautiful flowers. The overall scene facing the golfer on the tee—of colorful flora, blue water, green fairway, boulders marking the demarcation between the first and second water hazards, and a rugged desert mountain backdrop—is an arresting one.

As for the golf, the Tom Fazio–designed hole is a dogleg to the right, with water down the right side. The preferred shot is a fade; in fact, long hitters may go through the fairway if they hit it straight (they may prefer to lay up). A fade that turns into a slice is bad news, however. Even after a good drive, the approach must avoid another water hazard bordering the green on the front right.

The very exclusive Vintage Club hosted a tournament in the early days of the Seniors Tour. It was then that another great, Sam Snead, called it "one of the most beautiful and distracting holes in golf."

No. 12 Nirwana Bali Golf Club, Tabanan, Bali, Indonesia
↻
7th Hole, 214 Yards, Par 3

If you make a golf trip to Indonesia, you expect something exotic. You've got it here: Sitting just offshore and beyond the green of this par 3 is a tiny but dramatic island formed by a rock outcropping, atop which is the Hindu sea temple of Tanah Lot.

The hole itself is something special, too, on this resort course designed by Greg Norman and Bob Harrison in 1998. Like some of the other par 3s in this category, it plays across an inlet of ocean to a green perched on the other side. The local flavor here is provided not only by the temple but by the lush tropical vegetation lining the beach and forming the backdrop. The beach is not really in play short, as there is plenty of room in front of the green, though you may find a deep bunker. But the cliff to the left is definitely a concern, especially if the pin is cut on that side.

No. 13 Pacific Dunes, Bandon, Oregon

⌒

13th Hole, 444 Yards, Par 4

The 13th enjoys such a natural setting for a golf hole that architect Tom Doak says he suspects any golfer could have found it in laying out the course. To the left is the Pacific Ocean some seventy-five feet below. To the right are sand dunes, including a big one near the green that rises to a height of sixty feet.

While Pacific Dunes is not a long course (6,633 yards from the tips), the 13th is one hole that does challenge the golfer with length. That's especially true when it's playing into the wind, which is the prevailing direction in summer. And the wind can *really* blow here.

Going way left is an obvious no-no, but the accurate golfer will aim for the left portion of the fairway for a better angle of approach. A tee shot that strays to the right will leave a tough second shot over blown-out dune bunkers and a couple of man-made bunkers. The green is very deep and features a false front, so be sure to get the ball far enough onto the putting surface, or you will see it rolling back toward you.

No. 14 Kauri Cliffs,
Matauri Bay, New Zealand

◯

7th Hole, 221 Yards, Par 3

There are views of the ocean from no fewer than fifteen holes at Kauri Cliffs on New Zealand's North Island, including six that play along the cliffs at this high-end resort course. The course first reaches land's end at this beauty, featuring views of the distinctive, tiny Cavalli Islands that stand very close to the shore and come in a variety of shapes.

When you take your eyes off the seascape and look at the green, you're met with a sobering sight. The cliffs aren't as stark as those at some other cliffside par 3s in the world, being covered with vegetation, but the tee shot is no less daunting. It's long, with a carry of 200 yards from the championship tee to reach the relative safety of the front bunkers and 205 yards to reach the green. Playing from the proper tee is important on this hole; from the middle markers the carry over trouble is 155 yards.

The cliffs also await at the right of the green, with American architect David Harman providing only a few yards of leeway for missing the putting surface. Watch out: The wind very often blows toward the ocean here.

No. 15 Pinnacle Point Beach and Golf Resort, Mossel Bay, South Africa

○

8th Hole, 350 Yards, Par 4

The course opened only in November of 2006, but the accolades quickly started rolling in. George Peper, a veteran observer of the international golf scene, wrote in *Links* magazine that Pinnacle Point is "the most spectacular course I have ever seen." South African golf writer Grant Winter reached the same conclusion in *The Mercury* newspaper. European Tour professional Darren Clarke called it "the best golf course on the planet," though it must be disclosed that he is affiliated with the resort. More to the point is his description of Pinnacle Point as "Pebble Beach on steroids."

Pinnacle, like Pebble, is laid out atop cliffs overlooking the ocean (in this case the Indian Ocean; the course is a half hour south of George along South Africa's Garden Route). But here the cliffs are some 600 feet above the ocean. And no less than seven holes provide the thrill of playing over chasms to get from tee to green on this layout designed by South African Peter Matkovich.

Any of those holes could have been picked for this Dream 18, but we've gone with a short par 4 that tempts long hitters to have a go at the green straight across one of those chasms, a daunting but tempting downhill carry of some 275 yards from the back tee or 235 from the middle. Any attempt that is short or to the right is irrevocably lost, and for that matter it's a longer carry if you miss left. But if you possess the length to entertain the thought, it's a classic case of "no guts, no glory."

**No. 16 Greywolf Golf Course, Panorama,
British Columbia, Canada**

↻

6th Hole, 200 Yards, Par 3

This hole is like a combination of the cliffs of the 12th at the Challenge at Manele in Hawaii and the mountain setting of the 4th at Banff Springs in Canada. As at Manele, there is a sheer cliff to the front and left of the green. Here the shot is downhill and offers a little bit more leeway in front of the green, but at the back there is a drop-off instead of safety. Again, there is plenty of bail-out room to the right on this hole designed by Canadian architect Doug Carrick, but what fun is that?

The overall view is more like Banff Springs, with twin peaks towering over the green, but here the mountains are more forested than rocky, making for a rich green backdrop. The only thing that isn't green, aside from the very top of the peaks and the two greenside bunkers, is the rock formation in front of the putting surface that gives this hole its name: Cliffhanger.

No. 17 Cypress Point Club, Pebble Beach, California

☊

17th Hole, 393 Yards, Par 4

No. 18 Pebble Beach Golf Links, Pebble Beach, California

☊

18th Hole, 543 Yards, Par 5

When he's standing on the tee, the golfer's eyes don't know which way to look. There is the beauty of the ocean to the right, but also vying for attention is a grove of cypress trees in the middle of the fairway.

Those trees force a choice between going to the left of them or taking the shorter route to the right. That shorter path brings the water hazard into play, not only to the right on the first shot but also hitting over it on the second. The strategy has changed since Alister MacKenzie designed the course in 1928. Originally, the idea was to tempt the player to take the shorter route in order to be able to get to the green in two; the long way to the left generally meant taking three shots to get home. With the ball traveling farther these days, the left-hand option has become more favorable because more people can hit it long enough to get past the trees and have a clear shot at the green. The route to the right is shorter, but is so narrow that for many it is not worth the risk.

Exposed to the ocean as it is, this is one hole you don't want to play in a strong wind. When the PGA Tour used Cypress Point as one of its courses for the AT&T Pebble Beach National Pro-Am through the 1980s, it would morph from a relatively benign hole to statistically one of the toughest on the PGA Tour when the wind kicked up.

Standing on the 18th tee at Pebble Beach, you feel you are almost *in* the Pacific Ocean. That's because you practically are. A couple of years after the course's 1919 opening, somebody (it's not recorded who) had the brilliant idea of piling dirt on some rocks at the water's edge behind the 17th green to make a new 18th tee.

The purpose was to strengthen a weak par-4 finishing hole, which later in the 1920s was extended by architect Herbert Fowler into a par 5 by building a new green some 175 yards beyond the old one. The result was not only a better hole, but one of the more thrilling tee shots in the game. With the surf crashing only yards away, you must aim your tee shot over the beach, cutting off as much as you dare. The ocean catches errant drives to the left, but to the right bunkers and out-of-bounds stakes come into play if you bail out too far in that direction.

The hole continues to curve gently around the ocean for its entire length. A lone, tall cypress tree stands sentinel short and right of the green to give you something to think about on your second shot. The 18th has become an even better hole for tournament play now that players are hitting the ball farther, as going for the green in two—which involves risk on both the first and second shots—is more of an option.

HISTORIC
HOLES

If you're lucky enough to play on some of the game's championship courses, you have an opportunity to play on the same field where the great ones have played. That's something you don't get in other sports.

This Dream 18 takes us to holes where Francis Ouimet, Bobby Jones, Ben Hogan, Arnold Palmer, Jack Nicklaus, Tom Watson, Tiger Woods, and others enjoyed some of their greatest moments. If we're playing a chip shot from the left of the 17th green at Pebble Beach, who among us wouldn't pretend we're Tom Watson trying to chip it in?

Playing in the game's ancestral home of St. Andrews in Scotland offers a different kind of historical experience, the special feeling of playing on grounds that have been used by golfers for some 600 years. Or not far away, at North Berwick, playing on the game's most copied hole.

This course starts out where Arnold Palmer launched his famous charge and finishes where Phil Mickelson suffered his famous flameout. It's a challenging course, but not a backbreaker. There are some potential birdie holes out there, so you have a chance to make some history of your own.

Left: **No. 14 Newport Country Club, Newport, Rhode Island** ↻ 14th Hole, 209 Yards, Par 3 *See page 37 for description.*

	Par	Black	Blue	White	Gold	Red
1 Cherry Hills 1	4	404	348	319	294	294
2 Scioto 18	4	446	424	414	401	401
3 North Berwick 15	3	190	190	179	179	172
4 Myopia 4	4	392	392	360	360	327
5 Inverness 18	4	354	329	306	283	258
6 Carnoustie (Championship) 6	5	578	520	500	490	485
7 Augusta National 16	3	170	170	145	145	145
8 The Country Club (Composite) 17	4	381	370	363	363	361
9 Pinehurst (No. 2) 18	4	445	417	382	312	306
Out	35	3360	3160	2968	2827	2749

	Par	Black	Blue	White	Gold	Red
10 Prestwick 1	4	346	346	346	282	282
11 St. Andrews (Old) 11	3	174	174	174	150	150
12 Philadelphia (Spring Mill) 3	5	585	559	526	473	435
13 Merion (East) 11	4	369	369	349	349	330
14 Newport 14	3	209	189	172	159	159
15 Oakland Hills (South) 5	4	490	426	394	342	338
16 Muirfield 17	5	546	546	501	466	466
17 Pebble Beach 17	3	208	178	172	166	150
18 Winged Foot (West) 18	4	452	430	430	409	409
In	35	3379	3218	3064	2796	2719
TOTAL	**70**	**6739**	**6378**	**6032**	**5623**	**5468**

No. 1 Cherry Hills Country Club, Cherry Hills Village, Colorado

◯

1st Hole, 404 Yards, Par 4

Arnold Palmer didn't seem to have much chance in the 1960 U.S. Open when he stepped to the tee of what was then a 346-yard opening par 4 on the course designed by William Flynn. He trailed by seven strokes, and no one had ever come from that far back to win the Open. Palmer had other ideas. He was ready to attack the course, and knew that in the mile-high altitude the downhill first hole was reachable with a big drive. Never mind that there was a strip of rough in front of the green that needed to be negotiated and a creek to the right of the fairway, or that he had double bogeyed the hole in the first round and bogeyed it in the third using the same strategy of going for it off the tee instead of laying up.

Palmer lashed at his tee shot, which flew straight and true, bounced through the rough, and finished on the green just twenty feet from the hole. "Marching off the tee, I felt a powerful surge of adrenaline, maybe the greatest I had ever experienced," Palmer later wrote in *A Golfer's Life*. "By the time I reached the green, I knew something big was happening to me." He made a birdie, launching a charge that saw him birdie six of the first seven holes on the way to a 65 and a two-stroke victory.

The hole now plays fifty-eight yards longer, with a bit of a dogleg, so it's not possible to "do a Palmer" from the championship tee. Ironically, it was Palmer's own design firm that made the change prior to the 1978 U.S. Open. But if you want to walk in Arnie's shoes, don't go to the back markers on this hole, not even if you're a scratch player.

No. 2 Scioto Country Club,
Columbus, Ohio
18th Hole, 446 Yards, Par 4

Bobby Jones walked to the 18th hole of the final round of the 1926 U.S. Open needing a birdie to claim an outright victory. Since the hole then played as a 480-yard par 5, it was a reasonable proposition. Still, it was a hole where he had made a double bogey in the second round. This time, Jones crushed a drive that was measured at 315 yards down the fairway, knocked a mashie iron to fifteen feet, and two-putted for the victory.

When the Donald Ross course was redesigned by Dick Wilson in the early 1960s, a new tee was built to turn the hole into a challenging par 4, as it was becoming too short for a par 5 but could not be stretched.

For additional historical significance, Scioto is the course where a Golden Bear cub once roamed the fairways. It's where Jack Nicklaus grew up and learned the game, and also inherited a reverence for Jones from his father, Charlie, who had watched the 1926 U.S. Open at Scioto as a spectator.

No. 3 North Berwick Golf Club, North Berwick, Scotland

15th Hole, 190 Yards, Par 3

Many courses have a par 3 that is known as a "redan hole." This one is *the* Redan Hole—all others are copies of this template.

The 15th at North Berwick dates back to 1869, when the course expanded from six to nine holes. The designer is unknown. It's slightly uphill, with a green that is mostly not visible from the tee and slopes from right to left and front to back. The green is angled diagonally from right to left, with a deep bunker guarding the left side at around the midpoint of the green. There are also three bunkers to the right. A club member who had been an officer in the Crimean War said the hole reminded him of a redan, a French word (since adopted in English) for a V-shaped salient on a fort. All of the holes at North Berwick have names, so this one was tagged "Redan."

This type of par-3 hole was popularized by early American golf architect C. B. Macdonald, who liked to incorporate features of Scottish holes on his courses. Later architects also copied the design, some with exact replicas and some with approximations. A hole does not need to be uphill or have bunkers on the right to be considered a redan, but the diagonal nature and slope of the green and the placement of the left bunker are considered essential.

No. 4 Myopia Hunt Club, South Hamilton, Massachusetts

◯

4th Hole, 392 Yards, Par 4

Back around the turn of the twentieth century, Myopia was the most feared course in the country for U.S. Open competitors. Hosting four U.S. Opens between 1898 and 1908, Myopia accounts for three of the highest seventy-two-hole winning totals in history, including a ghastly 331 in 1901. At one of those Opens, a player is reputed to have putted off the green on the 4th hole—and lost his ball in a swamp.

The course, playing as it does at 6,539 yards from the back tees, is not *quite* so formidable with modern equipment. It's still a good test, though, and a classic design laid out by one of the club's own members, Herbert Leeds. The 4th is a hole that doglegs around a wetland to the left, and has impressed observers through the ages. English golf writer Bernard Darwin wrote in 1913 that the 4th and 5th "are two as good consecutive holes as can be seen at any course in the world." Some eight decades later, golf architect and observer Tom Doak said that the 4th "might very well be the best hole of its length in the free world."

No. 5 Inverness Club, Toledo, Ohio
☽
18th Hole, 354 Yards, Par 4

Normally, the deep bunkers surrounding the green on this hole aren't the place to be. So when Bob Tway found himself in the right front bunker on the 72nd hole of the 1986 PGA Championship, tied for the lead with Greg Norman, it didn't look good. That changed with a swing of the sand wedge, as Tway's ball landed softly on the green and trickled into the hole for an incredible birdie. When Norman was unable to match the birdie, Tway had the title.

The 18th at Donald Ross–designed Inverness is unusual for a finishing hole at a major-championship course in that it offers a birdie chance, albeit not usually the way Tway did it. In the 1957 U.S. Open, Dick Mayer and Cary Middlecoff both birdied it to finish one ahead of Jimmy Demaret (Mayer won a playoff). But with a snaky fairway that is not easy to hit even with a fairway wood or iron, the bunkers, and a sloping green, it's no pushover.

Norman, incidentally, found more reason to dislike this hole when the PGA Championship returned to Inverness in 1993. He had birdie putts touch the lip of the hole but fail to drop in both regulation and a playoff that he eventually lost to Paul Azinger.

No. 6 Carnoustie Golf Links (Championship Links), Carnoustie, Scotland
☽
6th Hole, 578 Yards, Par 5

Ben Hogan played in only one British Open, the 1953 championship at Carnoustie. In the process of winning the title, he helped make the 6th hole famous.

The most salient features of Carnoustie's 6th are the bunkers in the middle of the fairway and the out-of-bounds fence running all the way down the left side. Hogan, confident in his accuracy, took the route between the bunkers and the fence (a path that became known as "Hogan's Alley") instead of the safer route to the right. His reward was the ability to hit a 4-wood second shot just short of the green on a hole that then played 521 yards, enabling him to chip and putt for birdies in each of the last two rounds.

At 578 yards, the hole effectively plays the same for today's pros. Many of them can reach the green in two unless it is playing into the wind, but first they must thread the needle with their drive and also avoid a stream called "Jocky's Burn" to the right on their second shot.

No. 7 Augusta National Golf Club, Augusta, Georgia

୦

16th Hole, 170 Yards, Par 3

No hole at Augusta National has seen more highlight-reel moments than the 16th, a par 3 that was redesigned in 1947 by Robert Trent Jones, who turned a stream into a pond guarding the left side of the green. In winning perhaps the two greatest Masters, in 1975 and 1986, Jack Nicklaus had his signature moments on the 16th, sinking a forty-foot birdie putt in 1975 and hitting his tee shot to within four feet and making a birdie in 1986. In both cases, his chief competitors (Tom Weiskopf in 1975, Seve Ballesteros in 1986) were playing behind him and were unnerved by the gallery roar, following up by making mistakes that would ultimately cost them the tournament.

The Nicklaus moments are tough to top, but Tiger Woods did just that in 2005. Locked in a head-to-head duel with Chris DiMarco, Woods seemed about to drop a shot when he missed the green to the left (but past the water). Instead, he gained ground with a master stroke of a chip, which he played well to the left and past the hole, then watched trickle down the hill on the sloping green, finally toppling in on its last revolution. Woods went on to win in a playoff.

No. 8 The Country Club (Composite Course), Brookline, Massachusetts

17th Hole, 381 Yards, Par 4

With Lexington and Concord not far away, perhaps it is appropriate that this spot has been the stage for the pivotal moments in a couple of victories for Americans against adversaries from across the Atlantic.

In 1913, a twenty-year-old amateur named Francis Ouimet found himself in a contest with English stars Harry Vardon and Ted Ray in the U.S. Open. With Vardon and Ray already finished, Ouimet knew that he needed a birdie down the stretch, and he got it at the 17th hole, making a fifteen-foot putt. A heavy underdog in the play-off, Ouimet nosed in front and then virtually locked up the title by making another birdie at No. 17, while Vardon bogeyed after trying to cut the dogleg and instead ending up in the left fairway bunker. Making a great story even better, Ouimet lived just across Clyde Street from the 17th fairway.

Now fast-forward eighty-six years. The United States is taking on Europe in the Ryder Cup, and it's not looking good. The Americans have rallied from a four-point deficit to make it close, but it's getting near the end of the final day and it looks as though they might come up just short. But Justin Leonard caps a comeback against José Maria Olazabal by holing an unlikely forty-five-foot birdie putt on the 17th hole for the clinching point in a U.S. win, causing American captain Ben Crenshaw to kiss the green.

No. 9 Pinehurst Resort and Country Club (No. 2 Course), Pinehurst, North Carolina

◯

18th Hole, 445 Yards, Par 4

Golf at Pinehurst dates to 1898 and its No. 2 Course to 1901, but it wasn't until 1999 that the first U.S. Open was held there. It turned into a true classic, with Payne Stewart, Phil Mickelson, Tiger Woods, and Vijay Singh battling it out for the title in the final round.

By the time they reached the 18th hole, the contenders had been reduced to Stewart and Mickelson, with Stewart leading by one stroke. It's a straightaway but rolling par 4

to a green that, like all at Donald Ross–designed Pinehurst No. 2, has a lot of undulations. Stewart faced a fifteen-foot par putt for the win, and read the break correctly based on what he'd seen in a practice round. When the putt dropped, the gallery went crazy, having just witnessed the longest putt ever made on the last hole to win a U.S. Open by one stroke.

Adding intrigue to the situation was the fact that Mickelson's wife, Amy, was due to give birth any day. In fact, she had the baby the next day, when there would have been a playoff in the case of a tie. Adding poignancy looking back on it is that Stewart lost his life in a plane accident just four months later.

No. 10 Prestwick Golf Club,
Prestwick, Scotland

↻

1st Hole, 346 Yards, Par 4

No. 11 St. Andrews Golf Links (Old Course),
St. Andrews, Scotland

↻

11th Hole, 174 Yards, Par 3

Championship golf got its start at Prestwick with the first British Open (or Open Championship, as it is more properly called) in 1860. It was a humble exercise by modern standards, with a hardy band of eight players going around a twelve-hole course three times in a single day for a first prize of £10 and the championship belt. Willie Park won it with a 176 total.

The current 1st hole came into existence in 1883 when the course was redesigned and expanded to eighteen holes. Prestwick ultimately hosted twenty-four Open Championships, the last of them coming in 1925. That's the year Macdonald Smith, a transplanted Scotsman playing out of America, opened up a five-stroke lead through three rounds. The problem was that seemingly all of Scotland wanted to watch him, and in the midst of a swarm of hard-to-control spectators, Smith shot an 82 and finished in fourth place.

Most of the fans arrived by train on the railway line that runs the length of the right side of the first hole. After that Open, the governing Royal and Ancient Golf Club decided that Prestwick wasn't roomy enough to host the growing championship, and also decided to start charging admission to spectators to keep the crowd size down.

When you play golf at the Old Course, you are walking on ground where the game has been played since the fifteenth century. Now *that's* history. Nobody designed the Old Course; it just evolved as residents of the town took to the new game that involved hitting a ball with a primitive club toward a distant hole.

Bunkers such as the deep fronting Strath bunker and the Hill bunker to the left of the 11th green were not built, they simply evolved. They perhaps started out as small depressions where sheep took shelter from the wind, then became deeper as generations of golfers struck their balls from that gathering place.

The most famous incident at the 11th hole over the years involved nineteen-year-old Bobby Jones taking three strokes to get out of the Hill bunker at the 1921 British Open, and impetuously picking up his ball without finishing out the hole (he was already having a terrible round). Six years later, a more mature Jones returned to win the Open Championship at St. Andrews.

No. 12 Philadelphia Country Club (Spring Mill Course), Gladwyne, Pennsylvania

3rd Hole, 585 Yards, Par 5

The 3rd hole at Philadelphia Country Club's Spring Mill Course is historic in the same sense as is the site of a train wreck. When the U.S. Open was held at the club in 1939, this was the 18th hole (the order of holes at the William Flynn–designed course has changed, but the hole is essentially the same except for playing at 585 yards instead of the 558 it did then).

Sam Snead came to the final hole needing a par to win. But there were no scoreboards in those days, and he thought that he needed a birdie. That's what led him to gamble on trying to carry a cross bunker with a 2-wood second shot from the rough. In truth, it was a foolish gamble even if he had needed a birdie: It was a low percentage shot and he still would have had a reasonable chance at birdie by laying up short of the bunker. His second shot ended up in the bunker, from which point he made an even more disastrous gamble. He figured he needed an 8-iron to reach the green, but the shot didn't carry the lip of the bunker and buried in the face. He had no chance even to come close to the green from there, eventually reaching it in five strokes and taking three putts. The triple bogey will forever rank as one of the worst meltdowns in major championship history.

No. 13 Merion Golf Club (East Course),
Ardmore, Pennsylvania

ↄ

11th Hole, 369 Yards, Par 4

Two of golf's legendary figures staged their greatest moments at Merion. In 1930, Bobby Jones completed the Grand Slam (wins in the U.S. Open and Amateur and British Open and Amateur) at the Hugh Wilson–designed course just outside Philadephia. Jones's victory over Eugene Homans in the U.S. Amateur final, conducted at thirty-six holes of match play, was so convincing that he closed out the match on the 11th hole of the afternoon round in taking an 8-and-7 victory. Twenty years later, Ben Hogan completed his comeback from injuries suffered in a near-fatal car accident to win the U.S. Open at Merion, dragging his painful legs around the course in a thirty-six-hole final day that was a profile in courage.

The 11th is not one of the holes that was lengthened in preparation for the 2005 U.S. Amateur (the course will also host the 2013 U.S. Open), because its tee backs up to Ardmore Avenue. While it's a relatively short par 4, it can still wreak havoc owing to its devilish green site, with the "Baffling Brook" running in front of and to the right of the putting surface.

Bobby Cruickshank was leading the 1934 U.S. Open in the third round when he got what might have been one of the all-time great breaks: his approach shot bouncing off a rock in the brook and onto the green. Elated, he tossed his club into the air, saying, "Thank you, Lord!" but forgot to look up and had the club land on his head, knocking him to the ground. Unable to regain his composure, he shot 77–76 in the final two rounds and finished two strokes back.

No. 14 Newport Country Club, Newport, Rhode Island

◠

14th Hole, 209 Yards, Par 3

No. 15 Oakland Hills Country Club (South Course), Bloomfield Hills, Michigan

◠

5th Hole, 490 Yards, Par 4

Newport Country Club was not only one of the five founding clubs of the United States Golf Association, it hosted the first U.S. Open and U.S. Amateur in 1895. That occurred on a rudimentary nine-hole course that measured 2,705 yards, and the events were won, respectively, by English pro Horace Rawlins and American amateur C. B. Macdonald.

Newport expanded to eighteen holes in 1897 and later hired Donald Ross (1915) and A. W. Tillinghast (1923) to redesign the course. Only one hole remains pretty much as it played for the 1895 Open, the 208-yard 14th, which was then the 1st hole. It took a full-blooded drive to reach the green back in the nineteenth century, when the concept of par didn't yet exist. Now it's a long- to mid-iron played in the shadow of Newport's distinctive clubhouse.

See page 24 for photo.

There's history here, but it's not the kind you would like to repeat. Taiwan's T. C. Chen had a four-stroke lead coming to this hole in the final round of the 1985 U.S. Open, but lost that entire advantage by the time he left it. He found himself in the greenside rough after three strokes, and then perpetrated the most famous double hit in golf lore when his club made a second contact with the ball on his pitch shot, sending it to the other side of the green. That counts as a penalty stroke, and he completed the hole with a quadruple bogey. Shattered, he finished the round with a 77 and lost by one stroke to Andy North.

The hole also helped cost Bobby Locke the 1951 U.S. Open when he found a fairway bunker in each of the last two rounds and ended up in third place. Locke complained about the bunker being blind from the tee, but Robert Trent Jones, who had installed that bunker and many others in his redesign of the Donald Ross course, wasn't buying it. He reasoned that as long as Locke played practice rounds, that shouldn't have been a problem.

Jones's son, Rees, redesigned the course again in preparation for the 2008 PGA Championship and, ironically, regraded the fairway to make that bunker visible. But he also added thirty-five yards to the hole and tightened the bunkering around the green, furthering its status as one of the toughest holes on a tough course.

No. 16 Muirfield
(Honourable Company of Edinburgh Golfers),
Gullane, Scotland

⌒

17th Hole, 546 Yards, Par 5

The 17th hole at Muirfield demonstrates the fickleness of fate. In 1972, Lee Trevino and Tony Jacklin were tied for the lead as they played this hole in the final round, with Jack Nicklaus one behind and already finished. Trevino played it poorly, driving into a fairway bunker, pitching out, hitting his third into rough short of the green, and knocking his next shot over the putting surface. Jacklin, meanwhile, gave himself a fifteen-foot putt for a birdie. Trevino, appearing to believe that he had just thrown away the championship, hastily hit his pitch shot—and it went in the hole. A shaken Jacklin proceeded to three-putt for a bogey and then bogeyed the 18th hole, too. So it was Trevino, not Jacklin, who etched his name on the Claret Jug for the second time, and Nicklaus's bid for a single-year Grand Slam was quashed as he was coming off wins at the Masters and the U.S. Open.

No. 17 also played a role in Nick Faldo winning two British Opens at Muirfield. Paul Azinger led Faldo by one in 1987 until committing the cardinal sin of hitting his tee shot into one of the deep bunkers on the left of the fairway, the first step to what would be a bogey-bogey finish. John Cook had a one-stroke lead on Faldo in 1992 when he three-putted from thrity feet for a par on the 17th, missing a second putt of less than three feet. Faldo, playing behind Cook, tied it with a two-putt birdie on No. 17 and won it when Cook bogeyed the closing hole.

**No. 17 Pebble Beach Golf Links,
Pebble Beach, California**

᛭

17th Hole, 208 Yards, Par 3

**No. 18 Winged Foot Golf Club (West Course),
Mamaroneck, New York**

᛭

18th Hole, 452 Yards, Par 4

This hole that plays directly toward Stillwater Cove of the Pacific Ocean will forever be linked with Jack Nicklaus and Tom Watson. When Nicklaus won the first U.S. Open played at Pebble Beach, in 1972, his most memorable shot was a 1-iron into a driving wind at the 17th that hit the flagstick and stopped a foot away for a birdie to lock up the championship. Ten years later, Watson was tied with Nicklaus in a duel of titans when he chipped in for a birdie on the 17th to take the lead on the way to victory.

This hole is listed as 178 yards from the back tee, and that's the way it plays at the annual AT&T Pebble Beach National Pro-Am, but the tee is moved back for the U.S. Open. Even at 208 yards it's not exceptionally long, but the yardage can be misleading. The wind often blows hard in the player's face, and with the flag located in the back portion of the hard-to-hit hourglass green, it can be a fairway wood even for the pros.

Two of the most dramatic putts in U.S. Open history have been holed on this green. In 1929, Bobby Jones needed a twelve-foot par putt to reach a playoff with Al Espinosa, who had finished. It was a tough putt with a considerable break, but Jones judged it right and hit it just barely hard enough as it toppled in on its last roll. He would win the thirty-six-hole playoff by a whopping twenty-three strokes.

Greg Norman needed a fifty-foot putt for par in the final round in 1984 to stay tied for the lead, so it seemed that his best hope was for Fuzzy Zoeller, playing the difficult 18th behind him, to make a bogey. But Norman somehow holed the bomb and ended up in a playoff after Zoeller also made a par, but the effort was for naught as Zoeller took the playoff in a runaway.

The 18th really showed its teeth in the 2006 U.S. Open when Colin Montgomerie and Phil Mickelson both double-bogeyed it to lose to Geoff Ogilvy by a shot. At 450 yards, No. 18 is no longer fearsomely long, but both the tee shot and the approach must be precise on the A. W. Tillinghast design. Montgomerie messed up the approach to make his double and then, in the last group, Mickelson hit an errant tee shot to the left and had his second stroke hit a tree to let the Open get away.

EXCLUSIVE
HOLES

This Dream 18 is practically dripping with prestige, owing in no small part to the fact that the holes are located at ultraprivate clubs where it is exceedingly difficult for an outsider to play. But beyond the forbidden-fruit aspect, this is a truly outstanding collection of holes. These enclaves really do have something special inside those tightly guarded gates.

A few of these courses are well known, such as Augusta National. You've seen the 13th hole every year on television at the Masters, but chances are you haven't had the chance to play it. Other clubs keep a low profile 365 days a year. Two—Nantucket Golf Club and Fishers Island Club—are accessible only by ferry or private plane. Redtail and Morfontaine are located on little-traveled country roads. The most private of all is Ellerston Golf Course in Australia,

built on the private estate of the late Kerry Packer. It doesn't even have members.

Owing to the limited play these courses receive, along with the resources of the clubs' memberships, this Dream 18 is in exceptional condition. It features a collection of strong par 4s, from short ones to long ones. And it's the hardest course for women. In one instance—Garden City Golf Club—it's *impossible* for women because they are not allowed to play. A number of other courses on this list allow women to play as guests, but since there are no women members, there are no forward tees designed for them, making for some long holes. This includes Augusta National, Muirfield, Pine Valley, and National Golf Club of Canada.

Left: **No. 5 Fishers Island Club, Fishers Island, New York** ◯ 11th Hole, 164 Yards, Par 3 *See page 46 for description.*

	Par	Black	Blue	White	Gold	Red			Par	Black	Blue	White	Gold	Red
1 Chicago GC 2	4	450	442	442	427	427		10 Garden City GC 14	4	343	343	331	331	331
2 Redtail 6	4	370	370	336	336	336		11 Los Angeles CC	3	240	225	225	192	192
3 Nantucket 7	4	471	456	456	366	346		(North) 11						
4 Muirfield 9	5	508	508	460	449	449		12 Double Eagle 17	4	355	355	340	320	290
5 Fishers Island 11	3	164	157	157	154	149		13 Augusta National 13	5	510	510	455	455	455
6 Seminole 6	4	388	373	358	358	343		14 National GC of	4	460	445	420	397	397
7 Morfontaine 7	4	430	430	430	366	366		Canada 7						
8 Ellerston 16	4	456	438	438	438	402		15 Cypress Point 15	3	143	127	127	127	119
9 Ocean Forest 18	4	457	432	394	349	305		16 Shinnecock Hills 16	5	542	542	464	464	406
								17 National GL of	4	375	375	350	350	319
Out	36	3694	3606	3471	3243	3123		America 17						
								18 Pine Valley 13	4	486	442	442	427	427
								In	36	3454	3364	3154	3063	2936
								TOTAL	**72**	**7148**	**6970**	**6625**	**6306**	**6059**

No. 1 Chicago Golf Club, Wheaton, Illinois

◠

2nd Hole, 450 Yards, Par 4

No course has a more distinguished pedigree than Chicago Golf Club, which was founded by C. B. Macdonald, one of the pioneers of golf in the United States. Originally organized in 1892, the club moved to Wheaton in 1895—the same year that Macdonald won the first U.S. Amateur. One of five founding member clubs of the United States Golf Association, Chicago Golf Club has remained the most exclusive club in the Chicago area.

This was the first eighteen-hole course in the United States, with an original design by Macdonald featuring par-allel fairways similar to those found at St. Andrews, Scotland, where he had spent two years in his youth. The course hosted three early U.S. Opens, but needed modernization once the game advanced from its primitive early days in the United States. It underwent a complete redesign by Macdonald's protégé, Seth Raynor, in 1923.

Both Macdonald and Raynor often incorporated copies of Scottish holes in their courses, and the second at Chicago is based on the Road Hole (17th) at St. Andrews's Old Course. The similarities are mostly in the length of the hole, the angling of the green to the left, and a deep pot bunker guarding the left rear portion of the green. Long, narrow bunkers to the right of the green take the place of the road.

No. 2 Redtail Golf Course, Port Stanley, Ontario, Canada

6th Hole, 370 Yards, Par 4

The vision of a couple of wealthy Canadians, John Drake and Chris Goodwin, Redtail has only about eighty members and receives about 3,000 rounds a year. On any given day, there may be only a couple of foursomes playing the course, which is set well back from a lightly traveled rural road.

The course was designed in minimalist style by British architect Donald Steel and opened in 1992. Little earth was moved; there are fewer than thirty bunkers, and the greens are small. The 6th green is positively tiny at 3,300 square feet, a size that is possible to maintain in excellent condition only owing to light play. There are severe drop-offs on three sides and, what's more, a spine running down the middle of the green. Even with a short iron in your hands, it's not an easy target.

No. 3 Nantucket Golf Club, Siasconset, Massachusetts

○

7th Hole, 471 Yards, Par 4

In the nineteenth century, the island of Nantucket was a whaling center. Those days are long gone, and it is now an upscale summer retreat. And no place on the island is more upscale than Nantucket Golf Club.

The Rees Jones–designed course opened in 1998, but it is a throwback to an earlier time. The fairways follow the natural lay of the land and the greens and tees are close together to facilitate walking (there are no paved cart paths). The 7th hole is the hardest on the course. Not only is it a long par 4, but it is slightly uphill and plays into the prevailing wind. That wind can be strong—Nantucket's logo is a flagstick that is bent by a whipping wind. On "logo days," this hole plays more like a par 5.

No. 4 Muirfield
(Honourable Company of Edinburgh Golfers),
Gullane, Scotland

⌒

9th Hole, 508 Yards, Par 5

Muirfield makes this Dream 18 because it is the most exclusive course in generally egalitarian Scotland and because of the tales about its famously strict club secretaries keeping firm control on the gates (Payne Stewart was turned away one year, for example, when he showed up wanting to play). But it's the most accessible course on this list because it does open to outsiders on Tuesday and Thursday mornings (Stewart showed up on the wrong day, and unannounced besides). You might have to make reservations up to a year in advance and jump through some hoops of the club's devising, but playing Muirfield isn't an impossible dream.

The ninth at Muirfield is reachable in two shots, but they must be accurate ones. First, the fairway narrows in the landing zone for longer tee shots, with deep rough, bunkers, or out of bounds your punishment. The out of bounds, in the form of a stone wall down the left side, is even more in play on the second shot if you choose to go for the green. Shoot for an eagle at this hole and there's a real chance you'll end up with a bogey instead.

No. 5 Fishers Island Club, Fishers Island, New York

⌒

11th Hole, 164 Yards, Par 3

Isolation plays a major role in the exclusivity of this club, located on an island in Long Island Sound that is a haven for the wealthy. Though it is part of New York State, it is actually ten miles from Long Island and only two miles from Connecticut, from where it can be reached by ferry.

The course, designed by Seth Raynor and opened in 1927, features many water views. One of the prettiest is on the 11th, with its East Harbor backdrop. Vying for the golfer's attention, however, are a pair of deep bunkers on the left and right side of the green. And we do mean deep—the one on the left is twelve feet below the green surface! Of course, it's a relatively short par 3, so you should be able to hit the green. Right?

See page 40 for photo.

No. 6 Seminole Golf Club, Juno Beach, Florida

⌒

6th Hole, 388 Yards, Par 4

The rustic, comfortable locker room at Seminole is considered by cognoscenti to be the best in golf. While that is one of the highlights of the Seminole experience, the Donald Ross–designed golf course is pretty special, too. This is where Ben Hogan used to go to prepare for the Masters, and he was especially fond of the 6th hole, which he called "the best par 4 in the world."

Modern technology and today's driving distances may have taken away some of the sting of the 6th hole for the best players, but it's still an outstanding hole for the average player. The angled green offers the best approach to golfers who drive it to the left side of the fairway, but it's tough to stay on that side because the fairway slopes from left to right. That's probably why Hogan hit a right-to-left draw off the tee, followed by a left-to-right fade to the green, making the hole a shot-maker's delight.

No. 7 Golf de Morfontaine, Senlis, France

⌒

7th Hole, 430 Yards, Par 4

Built at the behest of the twelfth duc de Gramont by English aristocrat golf architect Tom Simpson in 1927, Morfontaine is consistently ranked as the best course in France. It is also the most exclusive, nearly impossible to play unless accompanied by a member. Only thirty miles north of Paris, it is nonetheless located in an out-of-the-way forested area and guarded by an iron gate, with a mile-long entry drive from there to the understated clubhouse.

Morfontaine has sandy soil and some design features of a links course, with one decided difference—trees, lots of them. It's a beautiful setting, and one of the most memorable holes is the 7th, where the drive is played over a rocky area to a fairway that slopes from left to right on a dogleg that turns from right to left. That makes it a difficult driving hole, but it is possible for a long hitter to cut the corner. The green has a false front and is guarded by a deep bunker on the left front.

No. 8 Ellerston Golf Course, Ellerston, Australia

16th Hole, 456 Yards, Par 4

There are private golf clubs, and there are private golf *courses*. Ellerston is one of the latter. This place is so exclusive that you can't even join it. The course was built in 2001 on the estate of Australian billionaire media magnate Kerry Packer. Packer died in 2005, but the course remains in his family's control and is played by only a handful of people a week. Some of them are the ones who rate Australian courses, and Ellerston is ranked as the number four course in the country by *Australian Golf Digest*.

Course designers Greg Norman and his associate Bob Harrison had their pick of anywhere on the 70,000-acre property, and they chose to feature Pages Creek. Ellerston is one of the toughest courses you'll find because, according to Harrison, "It was done specifically for the Packer family, and they can hit the ball." High handicappers should not be upset that they will never be invited to the course; they might never finish it if they got the chance.

Players need two solid shots in order to reach the 16th in regulation. The hole doglegs to the left around a ninety-degree turn in the creek, but it's impossible to reach the bend in the fairway with a tee shot. That means that with the creek flowing to the left of the green, the second shot must carry the water to get to the putting surface. It's an impressive scene, with the creek wrapping around the back of the green and a cliff face as a backdrop—a scene that will be seen in actuality only by a select few.

No. 9 Ocean Forest Golf Club,
Sea Island, Georgia

ↄ

18th Hole, 457 Yards, Par 4

Sea Island, Georgia, is home to the very high-end Sea Island Resort. Anyone can vacation there if they can afford it, but there's another spot on the island that you can't buy your way into: Ocean Forest Golf Club. Since the Rees Jones design was completed in 1995, it has opened its gates for the 2001 Walker Cup Matches and little else.

The 18th is the most visually stunning hole, playing along the Atlantic Ocean with the beach to the left all the way. That's a lot of sand to the left, but to the right of the fairway is a skinny bunker that stretches forty yards long and is also a place to avoid. Still, it's better to be on the right side of the fairway, because that gives a better angle to a diagonal green protected by two bunkers.

No. 10 Garden City Golf Club,
Garden City, New York

ↄ

14th Hole, 343 Yards, Par 4

Garden City is a tough course to get on for the average Joe. As for women—average or otherwise—it's off limits. Women are not allowed to play the course or enter the clubhouse, even as guests.

Oddly enough, this exclusive enclave on Long Island opened in 1897 as a public course, though that lasted only two years. The architect was Devereaux Emmet, chosen because he was a local golfer who had traveled to the British Isles. It was the first course of his career. The course was redesigned in 1908 by Walter Travis, a former U.S. Amateur champion who went on to design a number of outstanding courses. Both were Garden City members.

They left an architectural gem in the sandy soil of the Hempstead Plain, notable for its deep, well-placed bunkers. The 14th is a short par 4, but it becomes a tough one if you stray into any of the three fairway bunkers (two left, one right) or any of the seven sand pits around the small green. Most of those greenside bunkers are small, deep pot bunkers that do not allow an easy escape.

No. 11 Los Angeles Country Club (North Course), Los Angeles, California

⌒

11th Hole, 240 Yards, Par 3

It's not that far from Hollywood, but Los Angeles Country Club is not the place to go to find celebrities. In fact, actors are encouraged *not* to apply. One actor who did get in was Randolph Scott, but only after he had quit the movie business and become a businessman. Even so, he was told by one board member, "Randolph, we'd appreciate it if you would do what you can to keep your old movies off television." Ronald Reagan was another actor who became a member only after he'd gone on to other things.

Some consider Los Angeles to be the best course in the city, ahead of Riviera, but the members keep the course closely under wraps and do not host big tournaments. If they did, the 11th hole on this George Thomas–designed layout would be a challenge for anyone. It's a reverse redan green, with a drop-off and bunkers to the right. The good news is that the bunker on the left is well in front of the green, allowing a tee shot to land short on that side and kick down onto the putting surface. The Los Angeles skyline provides a backdrop for the hole.

No. 12 Double Eagle Golf Club, Galena, Ohio

◠

17th Hole, 355 Yards, Par 4

In the mold of Jack Nicklaus designing Muirfield Village near his hometown of Columbus, fellow Ohio native and Ohio State product Tom Weiskopf laid out Double Eagle in the Columbus suburbs (Weiskopf was born about two hours away in Massillon). Whereas Muirfield Village is a famous layout that hosts the PGA Tour's Memorial Tournament, low-profile Double Eagle was formed with the idea of a small membership and a low number of rounds. The two courses have one thing in common—both are included on most lists of top 100 courses in the country.

Weiskopf worked with then-partner Jay Morrish on this layout. As on many of Weiskopf's courses, it includes a driveable par 4; at Double Eagle it's the 17th. The 355-yard length is measured playing the hole as a dogleg to the left around a group of trees and laying up short of an expanse of sand. It's about 300 yards for a bold long hitter who is willing to skirt the trees and flirt with a lake along the right side. The green is huge at 12,000 square feet, which makes it an enticing target but means that hitting the green with a tee shot does not assure a birdie.

No. 13 Augusta National Golf Club, Augusta, Georgia

◠

13th Hole, 510 Yards, Par 5

Augusta National is one of the best-known courses in the world because it is the site of the Masters Tournament every year. Everyone is familiar with the 13th hole at Augusta from watching it on television. *Playing* it, however, is another matter. That's a privilege belonging only to Augusta National members and their guests. And if you're thinking of joining, it's a case of don't call us, we'll call you. There is no waiting list. Heck, you can't even get on a waiting list for Masters *tickets*, let alone membership.

The 13th, designed by Alister MacKenzie and club founder Bobby Jones, is one of the great risk-reward par 5s in the game. For much of its history, it played just 465 yards from the championship tee. Even at its current 510-yard length, it is very reachable in two for the pros (and even for some members at 455 yards). But the creek that runs in front of and to the right of the green has claimed more than a few victims, and the swale to the left is no bargain, either.

No. 14 National Golf Club of Canada, Woodbridge, Ontario, Canada

ↄ

7th Hole, 460 Yards, Par 4

The National Golf Club is hard to get on. It's also just *hard*, period. Known as one of the most challenging courses in Canada, the course record of 67 is held by Lee Trevino, who shot it at the 1979 Canadian PGA Championship. That was just three years after the course opened, but since then it has kept a low profile, as you might expect from such an exclusive club. Any thoughts of this course hosting the Canadian Open can quickly be dismissed, as its men-only membership does not square with PGA Tour guidelines.

The 7th hole fits right in at this demanding test that was designed by the uncle-nephew team of George and Tom Fazio. The drive must carry a forty-foot-deep gorge (keeping the ball in the air for 215 yards is required from the back tee), and then the players must negotiate the gorge themselves (there is no bridge). The approach shot is a long one to a green guarded by three large bunkers and fescue grasses waiting to grab a poorly struck shot to the left.

No. 15 Cypress Point Club, Pebble Beach, California

◠

15th Hole, 143 Yards, Par 3

Bob Hope once joked of Cypress Point that "one year they had a membership drive—they drove out forty members." That gives you an idea of the exclusivity of this club that enjoys perhaps the most magnificent setting in the game, where the Monterey Peninsula meets the Pacific Ocean.

The 15th is the first of back-to-back par 3s, a rare gambit that pays off handsomely at this Alister MacKenzie design. While the 16th and its long carry over an ocean inlet is more famous (and featured in Strategic Holes), the 15th is perhaps more beloved. It also plays over the ocean to a promontory, but it's a downhill short-iron shot to a green that is artfully surrounded by bunkers. The 15th is most testing when the flagstick is placed on a tongue of the green between a pair of bunkers on the right side, but no matter where the flagstick is located, the hole is an unadulterated pleasure for the senses.

**No. 16 Shinnecock Hills Golf Club,
Southampton, New York**

◠

16th Hole, 542 Yards, Par 5

Shinnecock Hills is not only one of the founding member clubs of the USGA, it boasts the first clubhouse in the country, designed in 1892 by Stanford White. Not only does it exude nineteenth-century charm, but it occupies a magnificent spot at the top of a hill overlooking a gem of a golf course.

Shinnecock Hills is as close as it gets in the United States to links golf. There is only one water hazard, but artful bunkering, fescue rough, near-constant winds, and well-deployed elevation changes provide all the challenge needed on this course designed by William Flynn and Howard Toomey in 1931 to replace an earlier version. The bunkering is particularly striking on the 16th, featuring a fairway that snakes between twenty bunkers, giving the golfer something to think about on each shot.

No. 17 National Golf Links of America,
Southampton, New York
ↄ
17th Hole, 375 Yards, Par 4

No. 18 Pine Valley Golf Club,
Pine Valley, New Jersey
ↄ
13th Hole, 486 Yards, Par 4

The lobster lunch is an experience to die for at this blue-blood Long Island club. So is the experience of standing on the 17th tee. It's one of the great scenes in golf, with Peconic Bay of Long Island Sound stretching out ahead, the magnificent clubhouse to the left, and this outstanding hole laid out in front of you.

It's a relatively short par 4 that plays downhill to a wide fairway, but it's one of the most beguiling holes in American golf. The best view of the green is from the right side, and for shorter hitters that's also the easiest carry over a stretch of sand separating the tee from the fairway. Fairway bunkers await the off-target shot on this side of the fairway, however. The safest play is toward the middle, but from there the shot to the green is semiblind. Holes like this one make the National C. B. Macdonald's masterpiece, as befits the layout that was his home course after he moved from Chicago to New York in the first decade of the twentieth century.

Pine Valley Golf Club is in a difficult-to-find location in the sand barrens of South Jersey, but don't worry—you probably won't ever need to find it. You can play only if accompanied by a member, and membership is by invitation only.

This course is ranked number one in the world by *Golf Magazine*, though it was designed by an amateur architect, founder George Crump, a Philadelphia hotelier. Pine Valley is exceedingly difficult for the average golfer because nearly every hole requires a carry over sandy, scrubby wasteland to reach the fairway. And while the fairways are generous in width, you're in deep trouble (sand or trees) if you miss them.

While not a long course for the scratch player or professional at 6,999 yards, the regular tees at 6,532 yards with a par of 70 are a stout challenge for a mid-handicapper. The 13th plays as a par 4 1/2 for most players at 442 yards from the regular tee. The direct line to the green for the second shot is a long carry over one of Pine Valley's sandy areas. For those who can't make the carry, or who just want to play it safe, there is a generous bail-out area to the right and short of the green, from where you can try to make a pitch-and-putt par. The expert golfer now faces some of the same challenge, since a new back tee has stretched the hole from 450 to 486 yards. While he might not need to lay up, the ace player has to be careful not to miss to the left, where a kick down a steep bank leads to big trouble.

HOLES
ANYONE CAN PLAY

Golf in the United States started out in the 1890s as essentially a private pursuit for club members. Decade by decade, it has consistently expanded into the public sphere, with more and more courses open to the public.

Early resort courses such as Pinehurst and Pebble Beach paved the way and by the 1930s they had been joined by New York State–owned Bethpage Black in a triumvirate of great public courses that still stands tall. Harbour Town and Spyglass Hill came along in the 1960s, both serving as sites for PGA Tour events.

The 1980s, 1990s, and early 2000s witnessed a major surge in public courses, many of them high-end daily-fee or resort layouts of high quality, albeit with hefty price tags. Prime examples are Pacific Dunes, which *Golf Magazine* rates as the number one public course in the country, and the Straits Course at Whistling Straits, which has already hosted a PGA Championship.

Of course, in the game's birthplace, Scotland, golf has always been a more egalitarian affair. Even the courses that are nominally private generally open up to the public on certain days of the week, an arrangement that works out nicely for traveling golfers.

One note on the routing for this Dream 18. Many golfers have lamented the fact that the stretch of seaside holes at Spyglass Hill comes at the beginning of the round instead of the end. That has been rectified here, with the 4th hole at Spyglass slotted as the 16th hole on this dream layout.

Left: **No. 7 The Links at Crowbush Cove, Morell, Prince Edward Island, Canada** ⟲ 11th Hole, 565 Yards, Par 5 *See page 62 for description.*

	Par	Black	Blue	White	Gold	Red			Par	Black	Blue	White	Gold	Red
1 TPC Sawgrass (Stadium) 16	5	523	486	486	470	410		10 Bethpage (Black) 10	4	502	434	434	377	377
								11 Pacific Dunes 11	3	148	148	131	114	96
2 Western Gailes 17	4	443	443	407	407	399		12 Bulle Rock 13	4	476	438	415	415	380
3 Pine Needles 3	3	145	135	126	126	110		13 Pinehurst (No. 2) 13	4	380	365	356	324	261
4 Black Mesa 16	5	536	494	480	433	364		14 Harbour Town 17	3	185	174	152	152	130
5 Nairn 5	4	385	377	371	371	281		15 Princeville (Prince) 15	5	576	576	525	525	410
6 Arcadia Bluffs 13	3	240	190	160	160	135								
7 Crowbush Cove 11	5	565	558	548	548	457		16 Spyglass Hill 4	4	370	358	345	345	299
8 Pebble Beach 8	4	416	416	389	369	351		17 Whistling Straits (Straits) 17	3	223	216	190	159	126
9 Barton Creek (Fazio Foothills) 9	3	175	155	135	120	106		18 Whiskey Creek 18	5	555	530	515	515	445
Out	36	3428	3254	3102	3004	2613		**In**	35	3415	3239	3063	2926	2524
								TOTAL	71	6843	6493	6165	5930	5137

No. 1 TPC Sawgrass (Stadium Course), Ponte Vedra Beach, Florida

↻

16th Hole, 523 Yards, Par 5

The Stadium Course at TPC Sawgrass does more than host the PGA Tour's Players Championship. For the other fifty-one weeks a year, it serves as a magnet for golfers of all stripes as the centerpiece of Marriott's Sawgrass Resort & Spa.

Architect Pete Dye created a spectacular three-hole finishing stretch. While the 18th is simply a hard hole, the 16th and the island-green 17th offer reasonable birdie chances while at the same time carrying the potential for disaster. The green on the par-5 16th is bordered on the right by the bulkheads of a water hazard, adding an element of risk for players attempting to reach the green in two or even to aim at the pin on a third shot after laying up. And it's no easy second shot even if you don't go for the green. The water hazard extends considerably back down the fairway, and a pair of trees on the left side means that the ideal layup must flirt with the water on the right. While the pros look at the 16th as a birdie hole, it's a birdie that has to be earned.

**No. 2 Western Gailes Golf Club,
Irvine, Scotland**

◠

17th Hole, 443 Yards, Par 4

**No. 3 Pine Needles Lodge & Golf Club,
Southern Pines, North Carolina**

◠

3rd Hole, 145 Yards, Par 3

Western Gailes is overshadowed by nearby Troon and Prestwick on the west coast of Scotland, but those who have found it consider it a hidden gem. Located on a narrow strip of land between the sea and the railway, Western Gailes is only two fairways wide, with nine holes playing along the sea and nine along the railroad tracks.

The 17th runs along the tracks, but a bigger factor is a large dune on the left that gradually narrows the fairway and, eventually, cuts it off. You need to hit a long drive that reaches the top of a ridge in the fairway in order to have a view of the green for the second shot.

The club was founded in 1897 by a group of Glasgow businessmen who wanted to play seaside, not parkland, golf. It was designed by a local greenskeeper remembered to history only as "Mr. Morris" (not to be confused with Old Tom). He did a fine job, as there have been only minor revisions through the years.

Donald Ross is well known for his creations at Pinehurst Resort, especially the No. 2 Course, but he did some fine work five miles down the road at Pine Needles, too. The 3rd hole is actually more picturesque than any hole at Pinehurst, a par 3 playing over a small pond to a green nicely framed by bunkers.

The water doesn't really affect the play of the hole—it's just a short-iron shot and the pond ends well short of the putting surface. The green slopes sharply from back to front, which means that a front pin position is the hardest. Trying to hit it close means flirting with the front bunker, but a safer shot leaves a tough downhill putt. Pine Needles, which opened in 1928, has become a favorite of the USGA, which held the 1996, 2001, and 2007 U.S. Women's Opens there.

No. 4 Black Mesa Golf Club, La Mesilla, New Mexico

꩜

16th Hole, 536 Yards, Par 5

Black Mesa is set on dramatic high desert terrain north of Santa Fe, with the fairways fitting in among sandstone rock formations, arroyos, and scrub. Nowhere did architect Baxter Spann work more artfully than in creating the 16th hole on this course that opened in 2003.

The 16th plays through a natural valley with steep, rocky hills on either side. The valley narrows at a couple of points, so that the fairway is only twenty yards wide. But the cautious player can avoid the bottlenecks by playing to the two wider portions of the fairway and then hitting a third shot to the green. Only the player seeking to reach the green in two needs to land his ball in the narrow parts, via a long drive and/or a second shot that bounces through the second tight-squeeze area to the vicinity of the green.

No. 5 Nairn Golf Club, Nairn, Scotland

⌒

5th Hole, 385 Yards, Par 4

While it's off the beaten path in the north of Scotland, Nairn is worth the trip. The site of the 1999 Walker Cup, Nairn was designed in 1887 by Archie Simpson, with later modifications by Old Tom Morris and James Braid. It was Braid who installed a bunker on the left side of the 5th fairway to tighten up the tee shot where the golfer already has to worry about the beach hugging close to the right side.

The second shot needs to be accurate, too, or it will be a difficult recovery from one of the three bunkers guarding the green or the drop-offs to the right of or behind the elevated putting surface.

No. 6 Arcadia Bluffs Golf Club, Arcadia, Michigan

◯

13th Hole, 240 Yards, Par 3

No. 7 The Links at Crowbush Cove, Morell, Prince Edward Island, Canada

◯

11th Hole, 565 Yards, Par 5

Arcadia Bluffs is one of the hardest courses in Michigan from the championship tees, with a course rating of 75.4 and a slope rating of 147. But if you play it from the proper set of tees, you should be able to get around. The 13th hole is typical in that regard. Architect Warren Henderson has created a monster from the back tee at 240 yards over a ravine. But it is well within the capabilities of the low handicapper from the next tee at 190 yards, the average player from the middle tee at 160 yards, and the woman or high-handicapper from 135 yards without a ravine carry.

The 13th does not require a carry all the way to the green, and it is downhill, but watch out about hitting it left. The farther left you go, the longer the carry, and a shot pulled more than a few yards left of the green has no chance of making it to safety. For those who take the conservative route, there is a bunker in front of the green at the right center. The hole sits on a bluff high above Lake Michigan, so the backdrop is something to behold.

The Links at Crowbush Cove, designed by Canada's Tom McBroom, put Prince Edward Island on the golf map when it opened in 1993. About half of the holes overlook the ocean, and overlook is definitely the right word for the tee on the 11th hole, which is located on top of a high dune, enabling a long view up and down the coast.

The dominant feature of the hole is a large wetland area that looms on the second shot. If you hit a poor drive, if the hole is playing into the wind, or if you are a short hitter, you might need to lay up short of the wetlands, leaving a third shot of more than 200 yards into the green. The hazard is on a diagonal, so there is the opportunity to go toward the left in order to shorten the carry. But if there's any doubt, laying up is better than hitting your second shot into the hazard, taking a drop, and playing your fourth shot from a long distance.

See page 56 for photo.

**No. 8 Pebble Beach Golf Links,
Pebble Beach, California**

ↄ

8th Hole, 416 Yards, Par 4

Pebble Beach has some of the highest green fees in the nation ($495 as of 2008), but holes like the 8th make the experience worth it. The 8th is one of the highlights of a seven-hole stretch along the Pacific Ocean that starts at the 4th hole. The view is spectacular here, and so is the golf.

Jack Nicklaus has called the approach shot at the 8th "the greatest second shot in the game."

That shot is played over a yawning chasm to a tiny green. Carrying the chasm shouldn't be a problem; in fact, some players will need to hit less than a driver off the tee to stay short of it. But the cliffs make for quite an impressive sight looking back from the other side. The ocean does come into play to the right of the green, but for the better player the difficulty of this hole lies in the small size of the target for the second shot.

No. 9 Barton Creek Resort & Spa
(Fazio Foothills Course),
Austin, Texas

ↄ

9th Hole, 175 Yards, Par 3

The Fazio Foothills Course, one of two designed by Tom Fazio at the seventy-two-hole facility, is the top course at the top resort in Texas. Opened in 1986, Fazio Foothills is a feast for the eyes as well as a good test of golf.

The 9th hole is a good example, playing over a ravine with a rocky waterfall on the left side and a bunker directly in front. The water hazard is a definite danger as it bumps up against the left front of the green. The timid golfer can bail out to the right, but the fact that it is a relatively short hole encourages golfers to have a go at the flag.

No. 10 Bethpage State Park (Black Course), Farmingdale, New York

)

10th Hole, 502 Yards, Par 4

Bethpage Black, the site in 2002 of the first U.S. Open at a publicly owned course, is known for having people line up in its parking lot during the night in order to get a tee time. Even after going to a telephone reservation system, Bethpage has preserved the whole first hour of tee times and one time per hour the rest of the day at the Black Course for walk-ups, to keep access to the course truly open.

The A. W. Tillinghast–designed Black is not a course for the faint of heart, the infirm (it's walking only), or high handicappers. It's formidable even from the middle tees at 6,684 yards, leading to the warning on the first tee that it is recommended for "highly skilled golfers." The 10th hole is a case in point. It plays 502 yards for the pros and 434 from the middle tees, and it's all carry to the green, which sits on the opposite site of a rough-covered depression and is guarded in the front by a deep bunker. To the left of the fairway are a series of bunkers and artificial dunes that give the hole the feeling of a links.

No. 11 Pacific Dunes, Bandon, Oregon

)

11th Hole, 148 Yards, Par 3

Tom Doak used the magnificent property adjacent to the Pacific Ocean to build an unconventional sequence of holes on this resort course, which opened to universal acclaim in 2001. The back nine has only two par 4s to go with three par 5s and four par 3s. Two of those par 3s come in a row, with the 11th the second one.

The 11th plays along the coastline, so the wind is a major factor, especially since the target is the smallest green on the course. The green is surrounded by native beach grasses, gorse, and bunkers, including a pair of extraordinarily natural-looking bunkers in front. It's not a hard hole on a calm day, but there aren't many of those in Bandon.

No. 12 Bulle Rock, Havre de Grace, Maryland

◯

13th Hole, 476 Yards, Par 4

The 1990s were the era of the high-end daily-fee course, and in 1998 Pete Dye turned out one of the best on an outstanding piece of property in northeast Maryland. It's known for undulating greens, thick rough (but reasonably wide fairways), Dye's usual visual intimidation, and hosting the McDonald's LPGA Championship since 2005.

The 13th hole is a standout, playing around a ravine on the right that is in play on both the tee shot and second shot. It's possible to play the ball out of parts of the ravine, but it's definitely something you don't want to do. The longer the drive, the better angle you will have to a green that is well defended by three bunkers.

No. 13 Pinehurst Resort and Country Club
(No. 2 Course), Pinehurst, North Carolina

◠

13th Hole, 380 Yards, Par 4

Pinehurst Resort has been one of the top destinations in golf since the early days of the twentieth century. It now has eight golf courses, but the biggest draw is the No. 2 Course, the one on which the most attention was lavished by designer Donald Ross.

Pinehurst No. 2 may lack a signature hole, but that's in part because it has eighteen excellent holes. The 13th is a fairly short par 4 that offers a birdie opportunity, but a potential birdie can turn very quickly into a bogey here. The green is elevated some fifteen to twenty feet above the fairway, which makes club selection difficult. If a player tries to get close when the hole is located on the front of the green and comes up short, the ball will roll all the way back down the hill to the flat of the fairway, leaving a tough pitch.

No. 14 Harbour Town Golf Links,
Hilton Head Island, South Carolina

◠

17th Hole, 185 Yards, Par 3

Harbour Town is the sole collaboration between Pete Dye, who was in his first decade of designing courses when the layout opened in 1969, and Jack Nicklaus, who was involved with his first course. It made quite a splash when it opened, largely because its small greens went against the grain of architecture at the time. Harbour Town, which is part of Sea Pines Resort, has hosted the PGA Tour's Heritage event since the year of its inception.

The 17th hole has a smallish green, but not a tiny one. It's one you don't want to miss, though. It drops off steeply on all sides but the front, with a long bunker to the left and two smaller ones to the right. Behind the green is the marsh that forms the backdrop of the hole. There is water to carry on the tee shot, but it shouldn't be a concern unless the shot is badly pulled to the left.

No. 15 Princeville at Hanalei
(Prince Course),
Princeville, Hawaii

◡

15th Hole, 576 Yards, Par 5

You don't have to be super straight to survive the 15th hole at Princeville at Hanalei's Prince Course—designer Robert Trent Jones, Jr., has provided a wide fairway. But if you uncork a wild one, there's a big price to pay, because the landing areas are nearly surrounded by ravines. The ravines are filled with lush vegetation and are pretty to look at, but not so nice if your ball finds one.

While it's conceivable that an ace player could reach this green in two, that would be an extremely rare event and the result of a perhaps foolish gamble. First, the long hitter might have to hit less than a driver off the tee because of a ravine that cuts across the fairway. Second, the green is guarded by a nasty pot bunker in front and is tucked close to a ravine on the right. There is much more leeway on the left side in the second-shot landing area, so that is the side to favor to set up a third shot to the green.

No. 16 Spyglass Hill Golf Course, Pebble Beach, California

◯

4th Hole, 370 Yards, Par 4

No. 17 Whistling Straits (Straits Course), Haven, Wisconsin

◯

17th Hole, 223 Yards, Par 3

Just up 17 Mile Drive from Pebble Beach Golf Links is another offering from the Pebble Beach Company, Spyglass Hill. Designed in 1966 by Robert Trent Jones, Spyglass starts out with five holes near the ocean before heading inland and into the forest for its conclusion. The land on those five holes winds through dunes and sandy waste areas, closer to a true links setting than the cliff-top Pebble Beach course.

The green at the 4th hole is unique, as it is very narrow but also fifty yards long. It's set at an angle to the fairway, so it is a very shallow target, with ice plant waiting behind the green. The hole bends to the left fairly close to the green, assuring that the second shot will be played over trouble. The fairway is narrowed by a fairway bunker on the right, leaving a choice of laying up to the wide part of the fairway short of it or going for the neck and leaving both a shorter shot and a better angle.

Pete Dye admits he designed Whistling Straits to be visually intimidating, and he emphatically succeeded on the 17th hole. There's some uncertainty planted in the player's mind because of a huge mound short of the green that blocks the view of the right half of the green. That focuses his attention on what he *can* see, which is the way the green is perched on a bluff above Lake Michigan, with a steep drop-off to the left side.

The safe play is to hit over the mound and hope to clear a bunker just short of the green on that line. If you go to the left, hope isn't quite lost. Despite the severity of the slope, the ball will probably get caught up in the long fescue grass or a bunker instead of plunging down to the lake. The bad news is that from there you will be doing well to get to the green in just one shot.

No. 18 Whiskey Creek Golf Club, Ijamsville, Maryland

○

18th Hole, 555 Yards, Par 5

There are other holes with double fairways and alternate routes, but none are quite as striking as Whiskey Creek's 18th hole. The fairway is split by the ruins of a nineteenth-century stone farmhouse in the landing area, and it's not there just for decoration. The narrower left portion of the fairway provides a shorter route to the green, giving long hitters a chance to get home in two, though they have to carry a creek in front of the green in order to do it. The wider fairway to the right sets up a second shot short of the creek. This is one hole where "down the middle" is one place you don't want to be, because you'll need to manufacture a shot around the ruins.

Whiskey Creek was designed by Michael Poellot in collaboration with Ernie Els, who went on to form his own design company after this successful project opened in the year 2000 northwest of Washington, D.C.

SHORT

HOLES

Can you imagine a "championship" golf course that measures 5,011 yards, playing to a par of 70? That's the case with this Dream 18, which includes a dozen holes on courses that have hosted significant professional tournaments.

Would it be a pushover? Hardly. Sure, every hole offers a legitimate chance at birdie, but plenty of trouble can be found. These holes require accuracy and, in many cases, a sound game plan as the player chooses among a variety of options. If you decided to go for everything on this course, you would be sure to get burned eventually. But if you didn't take any chances at all, you would feel like you were cheating yourself.

Well-designed short par 4s are often among the most interesting holes in the game. And while this course doesn't have much variety in distances, it does in the types of holes.

Many of the par 4s are reachable from the tee; a few are not (except perhaps for the longest hitters) because they play uphill or because of the placement of hazards. The ones that are reachable all feature risk as well as reward. And the best of them offer interesting choices for all levels of players from different tees, not just for the pro or scratch player contemplating whether to go for the green from the back markers. (The course measures 4,596 yards from the regular men's tees and 4,051 from the forward markers.)

Both par 5s, naturally, are reachable in two. Of the par 3s, the famed "Postage Stamp" hole at Royal Troon is actually one of the longer ones at 123 yards.

While classic old courses are well represented, six of these holes have been built since 1990. One of them, the 4th at TPC Boston, is a hole that was redesigned from a par 4 of more than 400 yards to one of less than 300. Sometimes, less really is more.

Left: **No. 6 Pebble Beach Golf Links, Pebble Beach, California** ◯ 7th Hole, 106 Yards, Par 3 *See page 78 for description.*

	Par	Black	Blue	White	Gold	Red
1 Westchester (West) 1	4	314	314	296	296	285
2 Ridgewood (Center) 6	4	291	291	275	259	259
3 Kingston Heath 3	4	296	296	296	230	230
4 World Woods	5	494	480	429	429	406
(Pine Barrens) 4						
5 TPC Boston 4	4	298	278	254	232	160
6 Pebble Beach 7	3	106	97	97	97	91
7 Olympic (Lake) 7	4	288	288	280	259	259
8 Royal Troon (Old) 8	3	123	123	114	114	118
9 Myopia 1	4	274	274	251	251	223
Out	35	2484	2441	2292	2167	2031

	Par	Black	Blue	White	Gold	Red
10 Riviera 10	4	315	315	301	275	275
11 Barnbougle Dunes 4	4	298	279	279	241	241
12 Royal Melbourne	4	305	305	281	281	257
(West) 10						
13 Merion (East) 13	3	127	127	121	121	114
14 Sand Hills 7	4	283	283	283	283	231
15 TPC River	4	296	278	247	247	226
Highlands 15						
16 Sperone 16	5	479	461	410	369	334
17 Doonbeg 14	3	111	111	106	95	83
18 Oakmont 17	4	313	296	276	259	259
In	35	2527	2455	2304	2171	2020
TOTAL	**70**	**5011**	**4846**	**4596**	**4338**	**4051**

No. 1 Westchester Country Club (West Course), Harrison, New York

◯

1st Hole, 314 Yards, Par 4

When the Walter Travis–designed Westchester Country Club hosted a PGA Tour event from 1967 to 2007, the nines were reversed, which means that this played as the 10th hole. But when the course is played in its proper order, it makes for an intriguing first-tee decision. Are you ready on your first swing of the day to gamble and hit a driver in order to try to reach the green if you're a long hitter (or get as close as you can if you're anybody else)? Or should you just safely hit an iron and start the round in careful fashion until you get limbered up?

Overall, the hole plays a bit downhill, but the last part is uphill after a plunge downward. The plateau just past the upslope and short of the green is a good place to be, which would mean laying up with a 3-wood for a long hitter or *not* laying up and hitting a driver for a shorter hitter. The main trouble to be found by going for the green is to the left, where there is a downslope leading to a bunker and trees. This was the first hole of a sudden-death playoff at the 1987 Westchester Classic when swashbuckling Seve Ballesteros went for the green but hooked his tee shot into a bad spot in the rough and made a bogey to lose to J. C. Snead.

No. 2 Ridgewood Country Club (Center Nine), Ridgewood, New Jersey

ↄ

6th Hole, 291 Yards, Par 4

There is not a lot of temptation to drive the green here. With the hole running uphill, the green ringed by bunkers, and the fairway ending fifty yards short of the putting surface, it's not a very attractive option for most. No, the thing that drives you crazy here is trying to figure out how it can be so darned hard when it's just an iron off the tee

followed by a wedge shot. It's no easy wedge, though, because it's uphill, which not only makes it semiblind but also takes some spin off the ball. That can make it hard to hold a tiny green that seems to repel shots.

When the PGA Tour moved the Barclays to this A. W. Tillinghast–designed twenty-seven-hole facility in 2008, it made sure to include the Center 6th in its Composite Course for the tournament (it played as the 5th hole). Some of the longer-hitting pros went for it, but generally only if they could reach it with a 3-wood. Trying to stop a driver on this green is like trying to stop it on the hood of your car.

**No. 3 Kingston Heath Golf Club,
Moorabbin,
Victoria, Australia**

⌒

3rd Hole, 296 Yards, Par 4

This course was laid out in 1925 by Australian professional Dan Soutar, and the bunkering plan was added shortly thereafter by renowned architect Alister MacKenzie on a visit to Australia. It's the bunkering that makes this such an intriguing short par 4.

A series of bunkers cuts into the right portion of the fairway, with two more guarding the right front of the green. This means that for those who possess the length to think about driving the green, or coming close to it, a left-to-right fade is necessary. But the green is a small target and the percentage play off the tee is a layup to the left side of the fairway, leaving a second shot of sixty to eighty yards.

No. 4 World Woods Golf Club (Pine Barrens Course), Brooksville, Florida

◠

4th Hole, 494 Yards, Par 5

Standing on the tee, you can see an immense area of sand dotted with scrubby bushes stretching in front of you, and the fairway as a haven of safety to the left. But the key to Tom Fazio's design here is that if you can carry that sand you can reach another portion of the fairway, and the green becomes reachable in two from there. Commendably, this feature is not only incorporated from the back tees, but also for regular players from the white tees, where the hole plays as a 429-yard par 5 (and also for low handicappers from a 480-yard tee and long-hitting women from 406).

Reaching the green in two requires not just distance, but precise shots. The gambler's fairway off the tee is narrower than the safe fairway, and the second shot must contend with a huge bunker on the right front.

No. 5 TPC Boston, Norton, Massachusetts

○

4th Hole, 298 Yards, Par 4

No. 6 Pebble Beach Golf Links, Pebble Beach, California

○

7th Hole, 106 Yards, Par 3

Until 2007, this hole was a 425-yard par 4, but an awkward one with a ninety-degree dogleg. When architect Gil Hanse and partner Brad Faxon redesigned the course that hosts the PGA Tour's Deutsche Bank Championship, their most radical change was to cut 127 yards off this hole and make it a driveable par 4.

It's driveable, yes—at least for the pros—but hard to actually hit the green in one. Only the extreme right side of the green is accessible, with the rest of the putting surface guarded by a large bunker. Even if you can successfully carry that bunker, there is little chance of holding the green. Still, the pros recognized that the area just off the green to the right afforded a much better chance for birdie than a layup, so in 2007 about 80 percent of them went for the green or its vicinity.

The shortest hole on this short Dream 18—it measures just ninety-seven yards from the regular tees—can be a pushover on a calm day, even with its small green that is practically encircled by bunkers. In such conditions, the overwhelming sensation standing on the tee is of the hole's beauty.

But the wind usually blows here, and when you add a 10- or 15-mph breeze, the 7th gets testy. If you amp up the wind to 35 mph, blowing into the players' faces as it was for the final round of the 1992 U.S. Open, it becomes an entirely different matter. The pros were punching 4- and 5-irons trying to keep the ball low, but very few were able to find the putting surface. Tom Kite didn't hit the green either, but his pitch-in birdie from the left rough was a key to his victory.

See page 72 for photo.

No. 7 Olympic Club (Lake Course),
San Francisco, California

⌒

7th Hole, 288 Yards, Par 4

This hole plays significantly uphill, so up until the 1990s it was reachable only for the longest hitters when the pros came to Olympic. With modern technology, though, it's in range for a lot of players. But actually hitting the green on this hole designed by Willie Watson and Sam Whiting is another story, as there are bunkers in front with a narrow alley between them. If you have the length to get to the vicinity of the green, the question is whether you want to try to get up and down from one of the bunkers or lay up short of them and hit a wedge from the fairway.

The biggest challenge here is the putting surface itself. It's very small, but nonetheless has three tiers, and a delicate touch is required. Many a player has three-putted and walked off wondering how they just made a five on what they thought was a birdie hole.

No. 8 Royal Troon Golf Club (Old Course), Troon, Scotland

8th Hole, 123 Yards, Par 3

This hole is known as the Postage Stamp because of its small green. In fact, the green is reasonably deep, but it is exceptionally narrow at about twenty-five feet. That makes it a difficult target even with a short iron, especially in the wind. The green is guarded by bunkers on both sides, the deepest ones on the right, so the narrowness of the green often leads to players blasting from a bunker on one side into a bunker on the other side, and maybe even back again. There is a dune to the left of the green that shields the flag from the wind, leading to confusion for players standing on the tee and trying to figure out where to aim or which club to hit.

This short hole causes problems for even the best players in the world when the British Open is held at Royal Troon. It cost Greg Norman the 1989 championship when the only blemish in a final-round 64 was a bogey on the Postage Stamp. He ended up losing a playoff.

No. 9 Myopia Hunt Club South Hamilton, Massachusetts

1st Hole, 274 Yards, Par 4

It's the shortest par 4 on this Dream 18, but not the most reachable with a tee shot. This hole climbs sharply uphill to a green that cannot be seen from the tee. It's a relatively straightforward hole, so players can tee off with whatever club they desire depending on their preferred length of pitch shot. Low-ball hitters, though, might want to use a club they can get into the air rather than trying to climb the hill with a driver.

Back when this hole was built in 1896, designed by Myopia member Herbert Leeds, it required two full shots for most players with the equipment of the day. That's no longer the case, but the severe slope means it still plays as a legitimate par 4.

No. 10 Riviera Country Club, Pacific Palisades, California

⌒

10th Hole, 315 Yards, Par 4

It's really not a percentage play to go for the green with your tee shot on Riviera's 10th hole. George Thomas designed the hole with the green angled from left to right, so it doesn't present its full depth when coming from the tee. The rear portion of the green is guarded by a bunker in front. It's a small target to hit from more than 300 yards away, and if you miss it you might end up with such a difficult pitch shot that you'll be happy to come away with a par. Still, it's downhill and just so tempting for those who have the length to get there. Then they hit one to the right or left of the green and wonder why they didn't just hit an iron off the tee.

The preferred layup is to the left side of the fairway because from that angle you are shooting at the full length of the green, and it's a pretty good birdie chance. The average player can play it even safer and hit it short of the bunkers that are 210 yards from the tee, but from there you're playing into a shallower green.

**No. 11 Barnbougle Dunes, Bridport,
Tasmania, Australia**

◠

4th Hole, 298 Yards, Par 4

Opened in 2004, Barnbougle Dunes on the island of Tasmania has quickly become one of the top public access courses in the world. Its must-play status derives from its wonderful linksland terrain and the imaginative design by Tom Doak and his Australian partner on the project, Michael Clayton.

The fourth hole is dominated visually and strategically by a large bunker set into a hillside directly on a line from the tee to the green. It's 237 yards to carry the bunker from the back tee and have a go at bouncing your tee shot onto the green, if you can avoid the bunkers left of the putting surface. It's a gamble not limited to scratch players; mid-handicappers might even be tempted with a 218-yard carry from their tee. The best area to lay up is left of the large bunker, which offers a good view and angle to the green. Laying up short of the bunker on the tee shot leaves a blind approach.

No. 12 Royal Melbourne Golf Club (West Course), Black Rock, Victoria, Australia

○

10th Hole, 305 Yards, Par 4

This hole is a dogleg to the left, so it has long been possible, even before the days of supercharged equipment, for a long hitter to reach the green by cutting the corner. You can only do so if you can carry a vast, deep bunker on the left side. Even if you get past that hazard, though, there are penalties for trying to drive the green and failing—trees and bushes to the left of the green, bunkers to the right, and a drop-off if you go long.

A long hitter who is shooting for a score is well served by joining the shorter hitters in playing an iron to the fairway and approaching the green from there. In match play, the gamble might be worth it on this Alister MacKenzie design.

No. 13 Merion Golf Club (East Course), Ardmore, Pennsylvania

○

13th Hole, 127 Yards, Par 3

The bunkers at this Philadelphia-area gem are called "the white faces of Merion." Designer Hugh Wilson, while otherwise incorporating Scottish touches on a course that opened in 1912, felt that bunkers should be visible, not hidden. None are more visible than the gaping front bunker on the uphill 13th hole. Here, it's the green that's practically hidden, a hard-to-putt green additionally guarded by three smaller bunkers.

The 13th fits into a narrow space between Ardmore Avenue, a fairly busy thoroughfare, and the clubhouse. So, while very few can get on the course at exclusive Merion, anyone can see this hole on a drive-by.

No. 14 Sand Hills Golf Club,
Mullen, Nebraska

◯

7th Hole, 283 Yards, Par 4

It doesn't play uphill and there is no hazard directly in front of the green. This means that many players can reach the green with their tee shot, or at least come close and leave themselves a short pitch shot, especially when the hole plays downwind.

They might come to regret the attempt, though. The green on this Ben Crenshaw/Bill Coore design is fairly small and there is a drop-off to the right. But the biggest reason for caution looms to the left and short of the green in the form of a huge bunker. The bunker's depth is eight feet, but not because it's dug that deeply into the ground. It is essentially built into a sand hill, with the bunker's top sitting well above the level of the fairway and green, serving as a highly visible reminder of the dangers of going for the green.

No. 15 TPC River Highlands, Cromwell, Connecticut

15th Hole, 296 Yards, Par 4

This hole at the course that hosts the PGA Tour's Travelers Championship is short enough that some of the pros can shoot at the green with 3-woods. It's definitely a birdie hole. But the key to this Bobby Weed–designed hole is the water to the left of the green. This brings bogey into play, and the possibility of big changes on the leaderboard adds excitement as the players head down the stretch. At just 247 yards from the regular tees, it can do the same for casual matches involving everyday players.

While the majority of pros go for the green or play just short of it, some hit an iron off the tee to completely avoid any chance of going in the water and/or to be able to spin an approach with a wedge. What you don't want to do is what Larry Mize did when he had a four-stroke lead in the final round in 1998—he hit his 5-iron layup tee shot to the right into an unplayable lie in the trees, made a double bogey, and ended up losing in a playoff.

No. 16 Golf de Sperone,
Bonifacio, Corsica, France

⌒

16th Hole, 479 Yards, Par 5

The only golf course on the island of Corsica, Sperone features an impressive stretch of six seaside holes near the finish of its Robert Trent Jones design. The best of them is this par 5 that bends around 100-foot cliffs overlooking the Mediterranean.

The biggest bend occurs in the last 100 yards, so any player tempted to go for the green in two shots must carry the water to get there. Sperone is a short course from the middle tees (5,959 yards), especially on this hole at 410 yards. So even the average golfer can experience the thrill of pulling off a daring shot to reach a par 5 in two, or the anguish of failing. The safe route, of course, is to keep your ball over dry land all the way, laying up with your second and hitting onto the green with your third. But is playing safe what you came to Corsica for?

No. 17 Doonbeg Golf Club,
Doonbeg, Ireland

14th Hole, 111 Yards, Par 3

No. 18 Oakmont Country Club,
Oakmont, Pennsylvania

17th Hole, 313 Yards, Par 4

The 14th at Greg Norman–designed Doonbeg requires a tee shot over a chasm to a green located on an oceanside cliff, but at this distance the carry is no problem. The cliff to the right of the green? That could be a problem. In fact, the long but narrow green is wedged between a tall dune on the left and the hazard on the right.

Like the 7th hole at Pebble Beach, the 14th at Doonbeg provides a spectacular view and is not particularly difficult when the wind is not blowing. But the Doonbeg hole plays even harder in the wind because the big-time trouble of the water hazard and the fescue-covered dune are so close to the putting surface.

The intrigue of this hole is epitomized by the fact that short-hitting Jim Furyk tried to drive the green in the final round of the 2007 U.S. Open and long-hitting Angel Cabrera laid up. The difficulty of the hole is demonstrated by the fact that both made bogeys. Furyk's was more costly, as he was tied for the lead coming to the hole but ended up losing to Cabrera by one stroke after hitting his drive to the left and catching a terrible lie in the rough. Tiger Woods, incidentally, also finished one stroke back, making only a par on 17 after reaching a greenside bunker with his 3-wood tee shot.

Oakmont, which opened in 1903 and was designed by founder H. C. Fownes, is known as one of the most penal courses on earth. The penalty on this hole is that if you try to drive the green and miss, you may be faced with a very difficult pitch or bunker shot. But it's a hole that entices you because it seems like a chance to make up some ground before a very difficult 18th hole.

LONG

HOLES

While this could be a true Dream 18 for the longest hitters, the "dream" label might be somewhat of a misnomer for those of more modest power. For some, it might be more like a nightmare.

Nonetheless, it's interesting to put together a collection of long holes to see what maximum scorecard numbers we can come up with for a legitimate par-72 course. The total: a whopping 8,748 yards from the back tees.

A decade ago, this course wouldn't have been quite so long. Any hole over 475 to 480 yards was automatically considered a par 5 unless it was extremely downhill. Now, with the increased distance achieved by today's equipment and stronger players at the elite level, par 4s can be stretched to 525 yards. This collection of holes also includes a 725-yard par 5 and a 288-yard par 3.

This is a pure course in that there aren't any holes that play as par 5s for members but are converted to long par 4s for tournaments. All of the par 4s play that way for all male players (three of them are par 5s for women). As much as possible, selections were made of holes that are long from all of the tees, not just the championship markers.

The majority of these holes are on courses that host professional tournaments. It does not come as a surprise that the majority of them have been redesigned in recent years to add yardage.

Since pure length was the primary consideration (along with selecting holes that have some character and are not merely long slogs), there are some holes that run significantly downhill and do not play as long as their yardage. Consider those the breather holes.

Left: **No. 1 Kapalua Resort (Plantation Course), Kapalua, Hawaii** ↻ 18th Hole, 663 Yards, Par 5 *See page 90 for description.*

	Par	Black	Blue	White	Gold	Red		Par	Black	Blue	White	Gold	Red
1 Kapalua (Plantation) 18	5	663	663	585	585	489	10 Merion (East) 18	4/5	505	463	411	411	395*
2 Cog Hill (No. 4) 18	4	505	448	396	396	365	11 Royal Troon (Old) 11	4/5	488	488	421	357	417*
3 Myopia 3	3	253	253	238	238	205	12 Torrey Pines (South) 12	4	504	477	456	443	394
4 Sunriver (Crosswater) 12	5	687	649	608	572	485	13 Old Head 13	3	258	227	203	176	120
5 SilverRock 15	4	525	480	453	425	399	14 Firestone (South) 16	5/4	667	583	583	583	353**
6 PGA West (Stadium) 6	3	255	223	187	146	133	15 Chambers Bay 14	4	521	496	450	407	309
7 Gallery at Dove Mtn. (North) 9	5	725	609	575	575	480	16 Carnoustie (Champ.) 16	3	250	245	235	223	212
8 Oakmont 8	3	288	225	207	207	185	17 Baltusrol (Lower) 17	5	650	570	543	525	448
9 Royal County Down 9	4/5	486	486	428	428	434*	18 Congressional (Blue) 18	4	518	466	425	383	379
							In	36/37	4361	4015	3727	3508	3027
Out	36/37	4387	4036	3677	3572	3175	**TOTAL**	**72/74**	**8748**	**8051**	**7404**	**7080**	**6202**

*Par five for women

**Par four for women

No. 1 Kapalua Resort (Plantation Course), Kapalua, Hawaii

◯

18th Hole, 663 Yards, Par 5

No. 2 Cog Hill Golf & Country Club (No. 4 Course), Lemont, Illinois

◯

18th Hole, 505 Yards, Par 4

What's this, a par 5 on this longest of Dream 18s that is reachable in two for more than a few players? Yes, the 18th at Kapalua has plenty of scorecard yardage but also 200 feet of elevation change downhill and a slope in the landing area for drives that approximates a downhill ski run. It is in range on the second shot for more than half the field when the PGA Tour plays its Mercedes-Benz Championship here, and possibly even for some mid-handicappers from the 585-yard regular tee.

The fairway on this Ben Crenshaw/Bill Coore design is extremely wide, but there is one thing to watch out for. When going for the green in two, a wild area of long, thick grass on the left comes into play. Hit it in there, and it's almost surely a lost ball.

See page 88 for photo.

This was a 480-yard hole until a 2008 redesign by Rees Jones—apparently 480 yards wasn't long enough to make a *really* demanding finishing hole. And since the goal is to convince the USGA to bring the U.S. Open to Cog Hill, a super-tough finish is what the course nicknamed "Dubsdread" now has.

It did not go unnoticed that the longer hitting pros were hitting short-iron second shots at the PGA Tour's Western Open (now known as the BMW Championship). But Jones did more than add length. He also moved the green closer to the pond on the left and, for good measure, increased the slope down to the pond. "I don't remember the last time a pro hit a ball in there," says course owner Frank Jemsek. "It should be in play now."

No. 3 Myopia Hunt Club, South Hamilton, Massachusetts

◯

3rd Hole, 253 Yards, Par 3

When Myopia Hunt Club was built in the 1890s, the concept of par did not exist. While this hole was a drive and a pitch at the time, designer Herbert Leeds had no thought that he was creating an easy par 4 or, for that matter, that it might become a tough par 3. He was simply making a hole of about 250 yards where players would make the best score that they could.

When holes started being labeled by par in the 1910s, this was a par 4. Eventually, without any changes except for the distance players were hitting the ball, it became a par 3. And a hard one, as it works out, because the green is fairly small—perhaps because it wasn't designed to be hit in one shot.

No. 4 Sunriver Resort (Crosswater Course), Bend, Oregon

⟳

12th Hole, 687 Yards, Par 5

This hole at the Bob Cupp–designed Crosswater is nicknamed "Endless," and it's easy to see why. It curves around a water hazard that runs the entire length of the hole down the left side, and does so in just such a way as to make it impossible to try to cut the corner at any point.

When the Champions Tour moved its Tradition tournament to Crosswater starting in 2007, it had some mercy on the over-fifty golfers and set up the hole at "only" 649 yards. More good news: With an elevation of 4,190 feet in central Oregon, the ball flies farther than it does at sea level.

No. 5 SilverRock Resort, La Quinta, California

〇

15th Hole, 525 Yards, Par 4

The course guide for this hole says that it "requires everything that you have to get home in two." While that wasn't quite true for the pros when the layout became one of the host courses of the Bob Hope Chrysler Classic in 2008, it did earn the distinction of being the longest par 4 ever played on the PGA Tour.

This Arnold Palmer–designed course opened in 2005 and was built for the twenty-first century at 7,578 yards from the back tees. As if the length of the 15th wasn't enough, there is a bunker inside the confines of the fairway in the right-center of the landing area and a canal that runs all the way up the left side, so you can't just whale away with impunity. Nor does the hole play significantly downhill. This is one hole you don't want to play into the wind.

No. 6 PGA West (Stadium Course), La Quinta, California

ↄ

6th Hole, 255 Yards, Par 3

The 6th at PGA West's Stadium Course is a Dye-abolical combination of length and water. It's not an island green. Not even Pete Dye would do that on a par 3 of this length. But standing on the tee, it almost *feels* like an island green.

Hitting the green requires an all-water carry to the putting surface. Also, any shot missing the green to the right will find the wet stuff.

There are two saving graces to this hole. The white tees are set at 187 yards, giving mid-handicappers a fighting chance. And there is a bail-out area to the left that serves not only those avoiding the water on the right but also the timid looking for a shorter carry to reach dry land.

No. 7 Gallery at Dove Mountain (North Course), Marana, Arizona

ↄ

9th Hole, 725 Yards, Par 5

How long does a par 5 need to be these days in order to be a true three-shot hole? With an elevation change of eighty feet downhill, it apparently needs to be 725 yards. That's what designers John Fought and Tom Lehman figured when they devised this hole in 1999.

For good measure, there is a desert wash crossing the fairway about forty yards short of the green, not to mention a 190-yard carry over the desert to reach the fairway from the back tee. But the most interesting feature of this hole is a lake that cuts into the right side, considerably narrowing the fairway once you get within 150 yards of the green. Playing your second shot safe to the wider part of the fairway makes it not only a three-shot hole, but a mid-iron third shot.

No. 8 Oakmont Country Club, Oakmont, Pennsylvania

ↄ

8th Hole, 288 Yards, Par 3

When Tom Fazio redesigned Oakmont before the 2003 U.S. Amateur, he stretched the 8th hole from 230 to 253 yards. But in preparation for the 2007 U.S. Open, Mike Davis, the USGA official in charge of course setup for that event, had an idea. Given that this was a hole where historically players had used woods or very long irons, he suggested building a new tee even farther back.

Davis knew that 288 yards would strike some observers as being over the top, but his reasoning was that this is a large, relatively flat green where a player can have a reasonable chance even from that distance. He was right. While it was certainly a challenge, the 8th did not rank as the toughest hole in the 2007 U.S. Open. In fact, it ranked only fifth.

No. 9 Royal County Down, Newcastle, Northern Ireland

◯

9th Hole, 486 Yards, Par 4

About 200 yards from the back tee, the hole drops sharply down by sixty feet. This makes for a blind tee shot—one of many at Royal County Down—but also adds welcome distance to your drive on this long par 4. Ideally, you want to favor the left side with your tee shot because it gives you a better view of the green. Be careful, though. Too far left and you end up on a gorse-covered dune. Drive it on the right side of the fairway and you will have to deal with a large dune to the right and front of the green on your second shot. Short hitters or those who hit poor tee shots will have to negotiate two bunkers fifty yards short of the green, including one in the middle of the fairway of this hole that was created in a 1926 redesign of the course by Harry Colt.

Incidentally, the vista from the point where Royal County Down's 9th begins its downward plunge is one of the most exhilarating in the game, with the hole stretching out below you, backed by the town, the sea, and the Mountains of Mourne. You might make a double bogey or worse, but it's the view you'll remember.

**No. 10 Merion Golf Club (East Course),
Ardmore, Pennsylvania**

○

18th Hole, 505 Yards, Par 4

Merion has always been known as a short course, but that adjective never applied to the 18th hole. At 458 yards, Ben Hogan needed a 1-iron to reach the green with his second shot to make a playoff (which he won) at the 1950 U.S. Open.

By the turn of the millennium, though, a 458-yard hole had ceased to be a long par 4 for the game's best players. So when Tom Fazio tinkered with the Hugh Wilson design, he added forty-seven yards to restore the 18th to its former shot values. The 2005 U.S. Amateur showed that it worked—for most players. A couple of young bombers managed to reach a downslope in the fairway with their tee shots, rolling to where they could hit short irons into the green. For most mortals, that's not a possibility. In fact, mid-handicappers are much more concerned about making the carry over the abandoned quarry in front of the tee to reach the fairway.

**No. 11 Royal Troon (Old Course),
Troon, Scotland**

◯

11th Hole, 488 Yards, Par 4

**No. 12 Torrey Pines Golf Course (South Course),
La Jolla, California**

◯

12th Hole, 504 Yards, Par 4

Until the 1997 British Open, this hole played as a par 5. When Troon made the switch, it didn't do so just for the pros, but also moved the regular tees forward and made it a par 4 for everyone. This way, everyone can face the same challenge of trying to make a 4 on a hole that is difficult for reasons beyond length.

It's called the Railway hole because a railroad lines the entire right side and is out of bounds. The railroad is more in play on the second shot because the green is snuggled close to it, and there are no bunkers to save you on that side. The hole is lined by thick gorse all the way down the left, but it's a Scylla and Charybdis situation off the tee, as there is gorse on the right in the landing area for tee shots.

The PGA Tour doesn't even play this hole at its full length at the Buick Invitational, setting it up at a mere 477 yards. The USGA listed it at 504 yards for the 2008 U.S. Open, though it did move the tees up a bit in a couple of rounds. There's nothing fancy about this hole, which plays straightaway with no water hazards. But its sheer length, combined with U.S. Open rough and strategic bunkering, made it the toughest hole of the championship, playing to an average of 4.585.

The Open came to Torrey Pines thanks to a thorough redesign by Rees Jones of the William F. Bell layout that originally opened in 1957. Jones took a course that played 7,055 yards and turned it into a 7,643-yard behemoth.

No. 13 Old Head Golf Links,
Kinsale, Ireland
◠
13th Hole, 258 Yards, Par 3

This hole runs uphill, so it plays even longer than its yardage. Nor is it easy to bounce the ball onto the putting surface; to do so you must find the opening between the pot bunker on the right front and a deep bunker on the left front. The shot for this hole is a lofted fairway wood or hybrid club to be able to get the ball in the air and land softly on the putting surface. That's if you even possess that shot. If not, at least you can enjoy the cliff-top view of the Atlantic Ocean.

No. 14 Firestone Country Club (South Course), Akron, Ohio

16th Hole, 667 Yards, Par 5

After the course was redesigned by Robert Trent Jones in 1959, this hole became known as "the Monster," not just because of its length (originally 625 yards) but also because of the pond in front of the green and the trees that line both sides of the fairway. Par 5s don't usually become famous for pars that have been made on them, but the 16th has seen a couple of memorable ones. On the way to winning the 1975 PGA Championship, Jack Nicklaus made a third-round par despite hitting shots from the trees on both sides of the fairway and taking an unplayable lie on the way. En route to the 1979 World Series of Golf title, Lon Hinkle intentionally skipped a shot across the pond and onto the green playing from the trees on the right side.

The downhill hole was beginning to lose some of its teeth until it was extended to 667 yards in 2003. Now it is once again one of the most formidable par 5s on the PGA Tour.

No. 15 Chambers Bay, University Place, Washington

⌒

14th Hole, 521 Yards, Par 4

Talk about being on the fast track. Chambers Bay opened in 2007 and within a year was named by the USGA to host the 2015 U.S. Open. The links-style municipal course built on sandy ground overlooking Puget Sound and designed by Robert Trent Jones, Jr., is that impressive. Nor does it hurt that it has the length to challenge today's bombers.

But the 14th hole is as much about strategy as distance. A player can shorten the hole by aiming at the left side of the fairway, but in order to get there he must make a longer carry over a large, deep sandy area known as the "pit of despair." Another large sandy area—not a bunker, exactly—awaits left of the green.

No. 16 Carnoustie Golf Links
(Championship Links),
Carnoustie, Scotland
◠
16th Hole, 250 Yards, Par 3

The 16th at Carnoustie is one of the toughest par 3s in the world for the pros, and it may even be harder for the average player who only gets a break of fifteen yards and has to play it at 235 yards. Nearly everyone will have to run the ball up to the green. The problem is that there are three bunkers on the right front and two on the left front, so the shot must be deadly accurate to avoid them and bounce up to the putting surface.

Even as he was winning the 1975 British Open, Tom Watson found this hole to be too much. He failed to make a single par in five tries, including a playoff.

No. 17 Baltusrol Golf Club
(Lower Course),
Springfield, New Jersey
◠
17th Hole, 650 Yards, Par 5

When A. W. Tillinghast designed this hole, he installed a huge cross bunker that would be difficult to carry after a poor drive, while making the hole so long that it would be tough to reach the green in three after laying up short of the bunker. That single bunker has now been divided into a series of smaller bunkers, but since there is still a break in the fairway, the effect is the same for the average player.

Today's pros, on the contrary, can usually carry the cross bunkering even from the rough. And the longest of them can even shoot at the green in two, even though another group of bunkers short of the green requires that the ball must be flown all the way to the putting surface. (Only John Daly was able to keep his second shot on the putting surface in the 1993 U.S. Open at 630 yards and again at the 2005 PGA Championship at 650.) Still, it's out of reach in two for most of the pros, and in today's world that's saying something.

HARD
HOLES

Tackling this course would be the ultimate challenge. If you're having a bad day, it would beat you up like no other. But imagine the satisfaction if your game was on and you matched your handicap or broke par.

These are not definitively the eighteen toughest holes in the world. For starters, there is no such thing—this is a subjective topic. For another, some holes that were strong candidates were slotted into other Dream 18s such as Water Holes (e.g., the 18th at Doral Blue) and Long Holes (the 6th at PGA West Stadium).

The main criterion was resistance to scoring, so this is quite a long course. There are certainly short holes that are exacting, but holes that combine length with the potential for disaster will produce a higher average score. You name it and these holes have it: water hazards, severe bunkers, severe greens, out of bounds, deep rough, trees.

Some of these holes, such as the 17th on the Old Course at St. Andrews and the 15th at Bethpage Black, have produced average scores of more than a half-stroke over par in major championships. Now *that's* tough.

Left: **No. 17 St. Andrews (Old Course), St. Andrews, Scotland** ↻ 17th Hole, 455 Yards, Par 4 *See page 118 for description.*

	Par	Black	Blue	White	Gold	Red		Par	Black	Blue	White	Gold	Red
1 Quail Hollow 18	4	478	445	381	347	306	**10** Bay Hill 18	4	441	427	414	391	277
2 Southern Hills 18	4	466	430	413	398	378	**11** Devil's	3	226	206	206	149	137
3 Fancourt (Links) 3	4	429	429	398	336	317	Paintbrush 13						
4 Oak Hill (East) 13	5	598	563	563	488	488	**12** Tralee 12	4	461	440	422	422	373
5 Pine Valley 5	3	235	235	219	194	194	**13** Medinah (No. 3) 13	3	244	181	181	152	152
6 Whistling Straits	4	489	435	413	403	370	**14** Royal Adelaide 14	4	489	489	423	423	365
(Straits) 18							**15** Bethpage (Black) 15	4	478	463	430	417	417
7 TPC Sawgrass	5	583	546	522	522	453	**16** Olympic (Lake) 16	5	609	579	579	507	507
(Stadium) 9							**17** St. Andrews (Old) 17	4/5	455	455	455	426	426*
8 Kiawah Island	3	221	197	182	168	122	**18** Carnoustie	4	487	444	428	411	383
(Ocean) 17							(Championship) 18						
9 Riviera 18	4	475	451	422	422	331	**In**	35/36	3890	3684	3538	3298	3037
Out	36	3974	3731	3513	3278	2959	**TOTAL**	71/72	7864	7415	7051	6576	5996

*Par five for women

No. 1 Quail Hollow Club, Charlotte, North Carolina

18th Hole, 478 Yards, Par 4

There are plenty of tough finishing holes on the PGA Tour, but since Quail Hollow rejoined the circuit in 2003, its 18th hole ranks among the toughest. In fact, in 2007 Quail Hollow's 18th ranked second behind Doral among finishing holes and was the fourth toughest hole overall at regular PGA Tour events (not counting major championships).

The George Cobb–designed course hosted the Kemper Open from 1969 to 1979 and the Wachovia Championship from 2003 to the present. In the interim, the layout was toughened up considerably in a 1997 redesign by Tom Fazio. The 18th was not only lengthened, but also shifted sideways to bring a creek into play. That water hazard runs up the left side and shifts to the middle after the tee-shot landing area, guarding the left front of the green before turning to hug the left side of the green. David Toms came to the 18th with a six-stroke lead in the final round in 2003, which was a good thing since he then made a quadruple bogey.

**No. 18 Congressional Country Club (Blue Course),
Bethesda, Maryland**

☾

18th Hole, 518 Yards, Par 4

This hole plays downhill, which is good news when you're trying to reach it in two shots. It was also good news for Ken Venturi at the 1964 U.S. Open, but for a different reason. This was the last year that the final day of the Open meant thirty-six holes, and on this occasion it occurred in temperatures approaching 100 degrees. Venturi suffered symptoms of heat exhaustion after his first round and, though buoyed by liquids and salt tablets, was barely able to walk the second 18 on the way to victory. If the 18th hole had been uphill, he might not have made it.

For most of the Blue Course's existence, this was the 17th hole though it was played as the 18th in most tournaments. After a 2006 redesign, it's now the 18th hole for regular play, too. The old Blue Course par-3 18th became the 10th hole, with the positions of the tee and green reversed. As for the "new" 18th, Rees Jones in his second redesign of his father Robert Trent Jones's course (the first was in 1990) added nearly forty yards to what had been a 480-yard hole at the 1997 U.S. Open. One thing never changes on the 18th—the water to the left and behind the green is very much in play.

No. 2 Southern Hills Country Club, Tulsa, Oklahoma

◯

8th Hole, 466 Yards, Par 4

The second shot at Southern Hills' 18th is decidedly uphill. What's more, from most spots on the fairway it is played from a downhill lie, which makes it difficult to get the ball up in the air. And it must be played with a mid- to long-iron by the pros, or perhaps a wood for the average player—the clubs that are most difficult to hit from a downhill lie. The target is a green with a false front where the ball will trickle back down into the fairway instead of staying on the front part of the putting surface. In major championships, you can add heavy rough into the equation. The only point of mercy on this Perry Maxwell–designed hole is that the creek that crosses the fairway just past the drive landing zone isn't very much in play, except that these days it might prevent the longest hitters from using a driver.

No. 3 Fancourt Country Club & Golf Estate (Links Course), George, South Africa

◯

3rd Hole, 429 Yards, Par 4

It looks like a links, but in fact the Links Course was artificially created out of a dead-flat former airfield by Gary Player and design associate Phil Jacobs in 2000. They not only conjured up the feel of links courses in Scotland and Ireland, they also built a world-class test of golf that has hosted such events as the 2003 Presidents Cup, the 2005 Women's World Cup, and the 2005 South African Open.

In Scottish style, each hole has been given a name, and the third is called "Calamity." The bunkers are deep here, but the toughest thing about this hole is the stone-walled "burn" that runs directly in front of a shallow green. This is one links hole where a Scottish run-up shot doesn't work. You've got to fly it to the green, but avoid rolling over the back of the firm surface.

No. 4 Oak Hill Country Club (East Course), Pittsford, New York

○

13th Hole, 598 Yards, Par 5

Other par 5s in the 600-yard range have become reachable in two by today's bombers. This is not so at the 13th at Oak Hill, where a creek crossing the fairway at the 300-yard mark forces long hitters to hit a 3-wood or less off the tee. If a player wants to get close to the green on the uphill second shot, he has to carry a large mound and two fairway bunkers that are on the direct route to the hole about 100 yards short of the green. Otherwise, he can lay up where the fairway bends to the left around those bunkers.

There are a couple of quick ways to make a bogey at this par 5 designed by Donald Ross—hit either of your first two shots into the rough or put your approach shot above the hole, leaving a treacherous putt.

No. 5 Pine Valley Golf Club, Pine Valley, New Jersey

5th Hole, 235 Yards, Par 3

The hole plays downhill, over a trout pond, and then uphill, but the green is above the level of the tee, making it play even longer than its yardage. That means the average player might need a driver from the regular tee at 219 yards. The worst place to miss is on the side where he is most likely to stray—the right. There is a steep drop-off to two bunkers and the woods beyond. It was from this area that

Gene Littler, fresh off winning the 1961 U.S. Open, made a quadruple bogey seven in a *Shell's Wonderful World of Golf* match.

The green is slanted significantly from back to front. While this serves to help a player stop his wood shot on the putting surface instead of bouncing over, he might not be so thankful when he faces a slick downhill putt. Club founder George Crump designed the course, but he consulted with architect Harry Colt, upon whose suggestion the 15th green was pushed back sixty yards from its originally planned location.

No. 6 Whistling Straits (Straits Course),
Haven, Wisconsin

ↄ

18th Hole, 489 Yards, Par 4

This hole has a huge green, covering 18,000 square feet and measuring sixty-four yards from front to back. That doesn't make it easy to hit in regulation, however. The Pete Dye–designed putting surface is shaped like a three-leaf clover with a long stem forming the front. The "wings" are well protected, especially the one on the left. A back location makes the hole play exceptionally long. The front stem is narrow. As for the center of the green, well, you're not likely to find the flagstick located there, and two-putting from that "safe" area to wherever the hole is located is not automatic.

The safer tee shot is to the right, but if you can make a 270-yard carry (from the back tee) you can take a shorter route to the left. Seven Mile Creek and a deep bunker guard the left side of the green. That bunker cost Justin Leonard the 2004 PGA Championship as he bogeyed to fall into a playoff, which he lost to Vijay Singh.

**No. 7 TPC Sawgrass (Stadium Course),
Ponte Vedra Beach, Florida**

↻

9th Hole, 583 Yards, Par 5

The hole takes a turn to the right after the tee shot, but the green is tucked a bit to the left just behind a grove of trees and a bunker. It's possible to get there in two shots, but only if your drive is long and favors the right side of the fairway. Even without any water around the green, the risk/reward equation is weighted toward risk, since the green is small and you can get in some bad spots in the bunkers and rough around the putting surface.

While the other par 5s at Pete Dye's TPC Sawgrass may offer birdie chances, the pros are content to walk away with a par on this one at the Players Championship.

No. 8 Kiawah Island Golf Resort (Ocean Course), Kiawah Island, South Carolina

○

17th Hole, 221 Yards, Par 3

With water hugging the right and front of a green that is set diagonally, cautious players will naturally tend to steer to the left. A miss to the left is better than one to the right, naturally, but pars will be hard to come by from there, with two deep bunkers and dunes to the left of the green.

The Ocean Course, designed by Pete Dye, gained a fearsome reputation when it was the site of the 1991 Ryder Cup, played mostly in a fierce wind. This hole made its mark at that event when Mark Calcavecchia punctuated a late-round meltdown with an ugly shot into the water and a three-putt for a triple bogey that allowed Colin Montgomerie to win the hole with a double bogey.

No. 9 Riviera Country Club, Pacific Palisades, California

○

18th Hole, 475 Yards, Par 4

The clubhouse at Riviera is on top of a big hill, with most of the George Thomas–designed course laid out in a flat area below it. The 18th is an uphill, sidehill march all the way from the tee to a green that sits in one of the game's great amphitheaters with a hillside to the left that is filled with spectators during the PGA Tour's Nissan Open (you don't want to be on that hillside facing a chip from Kikuyu-grass rough to a green sloping away from you). The great *Los Angeles Times* columnist Jim Murray once wrote that Riviera's 18th doesn't need an ocean to be tough because "it keeps the riffraff out with its bare hands."

Mid-handicappers often have a tough time reaching the green in two from the regular tees at 422 yards. Pros don't usually have that problem, but in the cold and rain of the 2001 Nissan Open, Robert Allenby needed a 3-wood to get home, drilling one of the more memorable shots of the decade to within seven feet for a winning birdie in a six-man playoff.

No. 10 Bay Hill Club & Lodge, Orlando, Florida

◯

18th Hole, 441 Yards, Par 4

The green at Bay Hill's finishing hole curves diabolically around a pond to the right of the putting surface, so that when the flag is located on the back right it is one of the scariest approach shots in golf. In that case, shooting at the flag means anything short of the back portion of the green or to the right will find the hazard. And the hazard is practically right up against the green, lined by an intimidating rock wall from which you seldom get a friendly bounce. From the fairway, practically all you see is water, rocks, and the flagstick.

Of course, you can aim at the center of the green, but the putting surface is pretty skinny, so a pull means that you find the bunkers to the left. And you can avoid needing to carry the water on your second shot by hitting your drive to the left side of the fairway. But there is out of bounds close on the left, which may be why during the PGA Tour's Arnold Palmer Invitational you see so many of the approaches coming from the right side. Golf legend Palmer not only hosts that event, he owns the course and has refined the original Dick Wilson design.

No. 11 Devil's Paintbrush, Caledon Village, Ontario, Canada

◯

13th Hole, 226 Yards, Par 3

This hole is a slicer's nightmare, as it hugs the course's boundary so that a miss to the right is out of bounds. Considering that the tee shot is a fairway wood for most players, that's a very real possibility. You also have to carry a deep swale to reach the green. Again, it's better to favor the left side, as the left portion of that swale is fairway and the right part is maintained as rough and dotted with a bunker. Architect Dana Fry has done you no favors on the green, either, which has two tiers and is difficult to putt.

Devil's Paintbrush opened in 1992, a couple of years after its sister course Devil's Pulpit (both are part of the private Devil's Pulpit Golf Association) east of Toronto. Very little earth was moved in creating the rugged Paintbrush, named for a wildflower found in the area.

No. 12 Tralee Golf Club, Tralee, Ireland

◯

12th Hole, 461 Yards, Par 4

There is heavy rough to the right of the fairway and a stone wall to the left on the tee shot, but the main difficulty on this hole is found in front of the green in the form of an eighty-foot-deep, rough-covered chasm. It's a long hole to require that a second shot be flown to the putting surface, which makes it play as a par 5 for many.

There is a narrow area to the right of the chasm where you could possibly lay up if you can't reach the green, but the more prudent shot is to keep short of it. But you don't even get a break with that attempt, as the fairway is extremely narrow at that point, with a dune on the right. If you fail to meet the hole's challenge, you can console yourself with the seaside views at this course designed by Arnold Palmer and Ed Seay, which opened in 1984.

No. 13 Medinah Country Club (No. 3 Course),
Medinah, Illinois

○

13th Hole, 244 Yards, Par 3

The first task here is getting the ball over the water in front of the green. While there is a slight buffer between the hazard and the green, a solid strike with a long iron or wood is not a given. Ben Crenshaw found that out at the 1975 U.S. Open when he hit a 2-iron into the water to blow his chances (the hole then played as the 17th). The next problem is that the green is wide, but not very deep, especially for such a long shot.

The back tee wasn't even used in the 1949 and 1990 U.S. Opens, when the hole was set up at 193 and 199 yards respectively, but given technology-induced distance gains, the pros can no longer expect any mercy. It played at 220 yards for Crenshaw in 1975, with Rees Jones tacking on the additional yardage in his 2002 redesign of the Tom Bendelow course.

No. 14 Royal Adelaide Golf Club,
Seaton, South Australia,
Australia

⌒

14th Hole, 489 Yards, Par 4

When Alister MacKenzie redesigned the course in 1926, he made it so that there were no longer any holes that crossed a railway line. But in recent times members began to see the 14th hole lose some of its bite, so back across the railroad tracks they went to build a new tee stretching the hole to 489 yards.

It's now a 273-yard carry to get past a cluster of six bunkers on the right of the fairway, three little ones in front of three bigger ones. What's more, the fairway narrows to a bottleneck in the vicinity of those bunkers. The hole then plays through a gap in the pine trees to a green that is fronted by a deep swale.

No. 15 Bethpage State Park
(Black Course),
Farmingdale, New York

○

15th Hole, 478 Yards, Par 4

This hole is so tough that the USGA didn't even use the back tee at the 2002 U.S. Open, and it still ended up as the hardest hole on a hard course. The tee had been built a couple of years earlier at the suggestion of Bethpage superintendent Craig Currier, added on after an extensive 1997–98 renovation of the A. W. Tillinghast gem by Rees Jones. But the USGA course setup officials felt the hole would be a sufficient challenge from 459 yards, and they were right—it played to a 4.600 average.

The hole plays longer than its yardage as the second shot is considerably uphill. For the pros, that makes it a blind second shot to a severely sloping green, but it's even tougher for the average player from the 430-yard white tees. When you factor in the upslope, the green is out of the range of many players, a difficulty compounded by the fact that the hill leading up to the green is covered with rough and bunkers. That leaves an unappealing choice of laying up eighty yards short of the green or hoping to catch a decent lie in the long grass or bunkers.

The Black Course is one of the toughest courses in the country for regular players from the white tees, playing at 6,684 yards with a slope rating of 140. As for the "ladies" tees, they are at 6,223 yards with a slope of 146. With four other courses at Bethpage, Tillinghast designed the Black for better players only.

No. 16 Olympic Club (Lake Course),
San Francisco, California

◠

16th Hole, 609 Yards, Par 5

No. 17 St. Andrews (Old Course),
St. Andrews, Scotland

◠

17th Hole, 455 Yards, Par 4

The genius of the Willie Watson–designed 16th at Olympic is the way it gently curves to the left for its entire length, making it a dogleg on both the first and second shots and rendering it nearly impossible to reach in two. Not that the average player is thinking about reaching it in two from the regular tees at 579 yards. Getting home in three would be just fine.

Reaching the green in three would have been welcome for Arnold Palmer and Payne Stewart in the final round of the U.S. Open in 1966 and 1998, respectively. Palmer hit his tee shot into the left trees and compounded the error by trying a risky shot from there that didn't come off. He ended up having to one-putt for a bogey. Stewart drove into the rough, ultimately causing him to need a 7-iron instead of a wedge for his third shot. He bunkered his approach and made a bogey. Palmer ended up in a playoff, which he lost to Billy Casper, and Stewart lost to Lee Janzen by one stroke.

Perhaps only at a course as old as St. Andrews, which evolved over the centuries rather than being designed, would a hole require a drive to be launched over buildings and an out-of-bounds area and then play to a green bordered by a paved road and stone wall that are very much in play. If a modern architect were to design such a hole, he would be denounced far and wide, but here it's tradition—and a very hard hole.

The buildings in question used to be railroad sheds and have been re-created on the grounds of what is now the Old Course Hotel. There's no way around it, the drive must be launched over them to reach the fairway. You can cut off some distance by aiming more to the right, but too far in that direction and you'll end up out of bounds. To the left of the fairway is the only deep rough in the center of an out-and-back course that generally features double fairways on its parallel holes.

There's only one tiny bunker on the hole, but it plays a role much larger than its size. The Road bunker to the left of the green is frightfully deep—it takes a great shot just to get out of it—and gathers balls from the left side of the putting surface. To the right is the road, from which the ball must be played, and the wall, which will interfere with your backswing if you bounce over the road. The safe way to play the hole is to leave your approach on the front of the green, taking the bunker and road out of play. Or almost out of play. Don't make the mistake of Tommy Nakajima in the 1978 British Open: He putted into the bunker, took four strokes to get out, and ended up making a 9.

See page 104 for photo.

No. 18 Carnoustie Golf Links
(Championship Links),
Carnoustie, Scotland

◠

18th Hole, 487 Yards, Par 4

Need we say more than bringing up the name Jean Van de Velde? The Frenchman famously needed only a double bogey on this hole to win the 1999 British Open, instead making a triple bogey that involved a trip to the Barry Burn in front of the green, among other misadventures, to drop into a playoff he would lose to Paul Lawrie. This hole burnished its reputation as a killer finish in the 2007 Open when leader Padraig Harrington found the burn twice on his way to a scrambling double bogey but still emerged as the winner in a playoff after Sergio Garcia, playing behind him, bogeyed from a bunker. Oh, yes, Andres Romero missed the playoff by one stroke after a bogey on 18.

Perhaps no hole in the world makes better use of a single creek (or burn, as it is called in Scotland). The burn guards both sides of the fairway in the landing area, thanks to making a horseshoe at that point. Then, after running up the left side, it cuts back across the fairway about ten yards short of the green. Just to make things even more interesting, there is out of bounds very close to the left of the green. The 18th is the work of James Wright, a local man who redesigned the last three holes in order to toughen them up for the 1937 British Open. He certainly succeeded.

WATER

HOLES

Bobby Jones pointed out that whereas being in a bunker is like a car crash, being in a water hazard is like an airplane crash—there is no chance of recovery. Curiously, therein may lie a good part of water's appeal to golfers. The danger adds an element of excitement to the shot, and adds to the feeling of satisfaction if it comes off successfully.

And, of course, the presence of water is aesthetically appealing. "It makes pleasant breaks in the course and generally the beauty of the surroundings pleases the eye," wrote architect A. W. Tillinghast in the 1920s. "The fact remains that water on the course is highly popular."

Water hazards were used sparingly by Tillinghast and other architects of his era. But since the late 1950s, when earthmoving became such a big part of golf course construction and architects were free to make ponds wherever they wanted, water has become a more prominent feature on most courses. Fifteen of the holes on this Dream 18 date from 1959 or later (the exceptions being Turnberry, Plainfield, and Oakland Hills). The apotheosis of the trend was the island green, a concept which came to life at the TPC Sawgrass in 1981.

A few of these holes offer views comparable to the Dream 18 for Scenic Holes, but the selection of Water Holes was based solely on how the water impacts the playing of the hole.

Left: **No. 8 Four Seasons Golf Club Punta Mita, Bahia de Banderas, Mexico** ◗ Hole 3B, 194 Yards, Par 3 *See page 128 for description.*

	Par	Black	Blue	White	Gold	Red		Par	Black	Blue	White	Gold	Red
1 Casa de Campo 17 (Teeth of the Dog) 17	4	463	433	377	360	288	**10** Blackwolf Run (River) 11	5	560	542	522	522	446
2 Hazeltine National 16	4	402	380	352	312	240	**11** Kingsbarns 15	3	212	185	151	151	110
3 Trump National Bedminster 6	4	438	410	381	351	306	**12** Plainfield 12	5	588	555	545	512	512
4 Kemper Lakes 17	3	203	172	142	142	82	**13** Royal Montreal (Blue) 16	4	456	421	405	357	314
5 Turnberry (Ailsa) 16	4	455	422	385	385	377	**14** Muirfield Village 14	4	363	336	325	325	269
6 Bay Hill 6	5	558	521	500	484	388	**15** Atlanta Athletic (Highlands) 15	3	227	204	175	145	103
7 Seignosse 17	4	401	401	388	388	328	**16** Oakland Hills (South) 16	4	406	406	380	374	312
8 Punta Mita 3B	3	194	189	184	179	175	**17** TPC Sawgrass (Stadium) 17	3	137	128	128	115	92
9 Glen Abbey 18	5	508	484	461	461	429	**18** Doral (Blue) 18	4	467	414	387	387	339
Out	36	3622	3412	3170	3062	2613	**In**	35	3416	3191	3018	2888	2497
							TOTAL	71	7038	6603	6188	5950	5110

No. 1 Casa de Campo (Teeth of the Dog Course),
La Romana, Dominican Republic

◯

17th Hole, 463 Yards, Par 4

Figuring that his 1960s creation Teeth of the Dog needed some new molars, architect Pete Dye returned a few years ago to renovate the course and add some new back tees. On the 17th hole, he went way back thirty yards to build a new tee that brings the water more into play on this oceanside hole. The drive must carry a healthy distance of water with a Cape-hole concept: A player can shorten the hole by making a longer ocean carry; a safer tee shot results in a longer second shot.

The ocean is just as much in play on the second shot, perhaps even more so because the target is a narrow green with water lapping near the right edge rather than a relatively wide fairway for the tee shot.

No. 2 Hazeltine National Golf Club,
Chaska, Minnesota
◯
16th Hole, 402 Yards, Par 4

In the original Robert Trent Jones design, the 16th was a par 3 that played near the shore of Hazeltine Lake without the water really coming into play. After the 1970 U.S. Open, the USGA told the club to change its 17th hole if it wanted to host another championship. The best plan was to change the 17th to a par 3, which led to a change on the 16th. As it happened, a group of four members tromping around near the lake found a spot for a tee. Then, beyond the original green, they found a spot for a peninsula green. Eureka! They had created one of the great par 4s in the game.

From the back tee, a carry of some 200 yards over water and marsh is required, with the hazard and a group of trees in play to the right of the landing area. The approach is generally with a short iron, but if the hole plays into the wind it's a dangerous shot with a longer club as the lake wraps around the green from the right front to the left rear. Just to complete the water-hole picture, Rees Jones, son of Trent, turned a drainage ditch to the left of the fairway into a well-defined water hazard in his redesign before Hazeltine hosted the 1991 U.S. Open.

No. 3 Trump National Golf Club,
Bedminster, New Jersey
◯
6th Hole, 438 Yards, Par 4

Of the four courses in the United States carrying the Trump name (the others are in New York, Florida, and California), Trump National Bedminster is the most likely to host a significant men's professional tournament in the future. The Tom Fazio design is a long course at 7,560 yards, but the 6th hole is a notable challenge without knocking you over with length.

The green is set on a peninsula. The good news is that the fairway bends to the right to get to that peninsula, so that if you drive to the left side of the fairway you won't have to carry water to aim at the center of the green. The bad news is that the banks of the green are shaved, so if you miss short, right, or long, the ball will roll down into the water.

No. 4 Kemper Lakes Golf Club, Kildeer, Illinois

17th Hole, 203 Yards, Par 3

There is water, water, everywhere at the appropriately named Kemper Lakes, and nowhere does it feature more prominently than at the 17th hole. The tee shot is all carry over one of the lakes that gives the course its name, and the green is situated so that water guards the left and rear of the putting surface as well.

Kemper Lakes, designed by Ken Killian and Dick Nugent, recently went private after having been a high-end daily-fee course since its 1978 opening. The course had its moment in the sun when it was the site of the 1989 PGA Championship, and the 17th was the hole that cost Mike Reid the title as he double-bogeyed it and lost by one stroke to Payne Stewart. The double bogey did not come as the result of a ball in the water, but from the highly contoured green as Reid hit a poor chip and then took three putts from fifteen feet.

No. 5 Turnberry Resort (Ailsa Course), Turnberry, Scotland

↻

16th Hole, 455 Yards, Par 4

In preparation for the 2009 British Open, this hole was lengthened by about fifty yards and turned from a straightaway hole into a dogleg right by shifting the fairway to the left in a change supervised by Peter Dawson, chief executive of the Royal and Ancient Golf Club, which runs the Open. It may not have made it a better hole, but did make it a harder one.

The most striking feature remains the same, a dramatic-looking burn that runs hard by the front and right of the green. The burn is narrow, but sits some ten feet below the green surface, at the bottom of a steep bank that serves to funnel imprecise shots into the hazard below. The angle of the approach shot is different since the redesign, but more significantly, it is played with a longer club, so more shots find the dreaded burn.

No. 6 Bay Hill Club & Lodge, Orlando, Florida

↻

6th Hole, 558 Yards, Par 5

The 6th at Dick Wilson–designed Bay Hill forms a reverse-C curve around a pond for its entire length, making it tough to reach in two. The carry is too long to cut off much distance on the tee shot, and then the second must fly all the way to the green if it is to reach the putting surface instead of getting wet.

This hole extracted an 18 from John Daly in the final round of the Bay Hill Invitational in 1998, and it didn't even come from shooting at the green à la *Tin Cup*. The game's most volatile player hooked his drive into the water, walked thirty yards forward to take his penalty drop(s), and proceeded to hit five consecutive 3-woods into the pond.

**No. 7 Golf de Seignosse,
Seignosse, France**

◑

17th Hole, 401 Yards, Par 4

Located near Biarritz, this Robert von Hagge design dates from 1989 and is a scenic woodlands course punctuated with several striking water holes. The best of them is the 17th, which doesn't have, or need, any bunkers.

The hole doglegs to the left around a pond that starts at about the landing area for a long drive, so if you're worried about hooking the ball, you might hit less than a driver. Don't leave yourself too long a shot into the green, though, as it is a narrow target perched on the edge of the water to the left, with a carry required because of the angle.

No. 8 Four Seasons Golf Club Punta Mita, Bahia de Banderas, Mexico

ↄ

Hole 3B, 194 Yards, Par 3

No. 9 Glen Abbey Golf Club, Oakville, Ontario, Canada

ↄ

18th Hole, 508 Yards, Par 5

The most natural island green in the world is located at Punta Mita, about an hour north of Puerto Vallarta on Banderas Bay. When Jack Nicklaus and his team were designing the Punta Mita course, they noticed an island about 170 yards off the coast. They also noticed that there were tall rocks on the back side of the island that served to keep salt spray off the rest of it. The wheels started turning in their heads. . . . The distance was perfect for a par 3, and no salt spray meant that grass could grow and be maintained. Voilà! Hole 3B was born.

There is a Hole 3A, which stays on the mainland, for those unable to make the carry. But the majority of players prefer to take a shot at the green at the unique 3B. At low tide, you can use a stone walkway to reach the green by foot. At other times you ride an amphibian vehicle driven by a member of the resort staff.

See page 120 for photo.

This is a short par 5 with a water hazard that is well situated for risk-reward scenarios. The Jack Nicklaus design features an angled pond that must be carried in order to hit the green with a second shot, and also will swallow up anything to the right. There is a bail-out area to the left, but there are bunkers and rough-covered mounds over there that make it quite unappealing.

The course, which opened in 1976, has been the scene of many Canadian Opens, none with a more exciting finish than 2000, when Tiger Woods hit one of the greatest shots of his career. He was in a fairway bunker 218 yards from the hole and was leading Grant Waite by one stroke. Waite, though, had already hit the green in two, so Woods decided to fire at the dangerous back right pin with a 6-iron that would have to clear the lip of the bunker and make a carry of more than two hundred yards. He did it perfectly, and two-putted from the back fringe for a winning birdie.

No. 10 Blackwolf Run (River Course), Kohler, Wisconsin

⌒

11th Hole, 560 Yards, Par 5

This course borders the Sheboygan River, and architect Pete Dye made great use of it on the 11th hole. The river makes a bend to the right at this point, and Dye built a par 5 around it that gives a variety of options on the second shot. The player can try to make a long river carry to get close to or on the green (the hole doesn't play as long as its listed yardage when that route is taken), or not carry the river at all and leave about a 150-yard third shot.

There are a couple of diabolical extra factors. First, there is also a water hazard to the left that comes into play for long drivers or on the second shot for those who have hit a poor drive. Second, there is a lone, large tree next to the river that blocks a possible second-shot route. It's either take the long way to the right of it or the short way to the left.

**No. 11 Kingsbarns Golf Links,
Kingsbarns, Scotland**

15th Hole, 212 Yards, Par 3

The sea never comes into play at the Old Course at St. Andrews, but it emphatically does about six miles up the road at Kingsbarns, especially on this par 3. The green sits on a spit of land that juts out into the sea, creating a tee shot that must be played over the water to get to the putting surface. The backdrop for the hole is nothing but water on the most picturesque hole on this Kyle Phillips–designed course that opened to much acclaim in 2000.

Since this is Scotland, the wind is definitely a factor, and even more so on this exposed extremity of the land. But, unusually for a links course, there are trees adjacent to the tee. They can block the wind and make it appear calmer than it really is.

No. 12 Plainfield Country Club,
Edison, New Jersey

◠

12th Hole, 588 Yards, Par 5

You don't often see a water hazard in the center of a hole, probably for good reason. But Donald Ross makes it work at Plainfield's 12th, creating a hole with strategic interest. The hazard in question is a narrow creek that comes in from the right at about 135 yards from the green. It starts out on a diagonal, then makes a turn and runs right straight down the middle of what has become a double fairway. When it nears the green, the creek turns left and runs past the left side of the putting surface.

The player who has hit a long enough drive to comfortably carry the creek and go for the right fairway can consider that option, which may or may not be the best choice depending on the hole location. But the creek is not only strategic, it is penal, too. If your shot to either of the fairways strays off-line, you could find the hazard. Thus, one more option is to play short of the creek, leaving a longer third shot.

No. 13 Royal Montreal Golf Club (Blue Course), Ile Bizard, Quebec, Canada

◠

16th Hole, 456 Yards, Par 4

Royal Montreal is the oldest golf club in America, having been founded in 1873, but moved to its present site in 1959. The Dick Wilson–designed course, renovated by Rees Jones in 2004, tests players' accuracy in the finishing stretch with the last five holes all playing over or adjacent to ponds. The 14th hole became famous at the 2007 Presidents Cup when Woody Austin of the U.S. team fell backward into the water after hitting a shot from the edge of the pond.

The 16th hole has its own entertaining story. In the 1975 Canadian Open, Pat Fitzsimons hooked his tee shot into the pond left of the fairway. Well, not exactly *into*. The ball actually came to rest on a small island about ten yards from the shore. The U.S. pro saved himself a penalty stroke and made a par by wading to the island through water that got as deep as his waist, and hitting his ball to the green.

No. 14 Muirfield Village Golf Club, Dublin, Ohio

◠

14th Hole, 363 Yards, Par 4

A creek angles across this fairway, starting at about 245 yards from the back tee on the left side and going to about 270 yards on the right. In the early days of the Memorial Tournament at the course that Jack Nicklaus designed near his hometown of Columbus in 1974, that meant an automatic layup off the tee. In the modern age, pros can consider carrying the hazard, but the vast majority still choose to hit an iron short of it.

That's to ensure that they will be hitting from the fairway and with the best angle for a second shot that is very demanding, even with a wedge. The creek continues along the right side to guard a green that is very deep but exceptionally narrow. There are two big bunkers to the left of the green from which even the highly skilled pros must worry a little about blasting into the water on the other side.

No. 15 Atlanta Athletic Club (Highlands Course), Duluth, Georgia

◡

15th Hole, 227 Yards, Par 3

It's all carry to the green here, except for the extreme left side of a putting surface that mostly sits behind the wooden bulkheads of a large pond. Since the green is on a diagonal, it's a longer carry the farther right you go and anything to the right is in the water.

The tee shot is downhill, but that's a mixed blessing as the better view of the water serves to make it even more intimidating. It will be scary even for the pros from the alternate back tee at 260 yards, installed by Rees Jones in his latest redesign and expected to be used only for championships. The hole played at 227 yards when eventual winner David Toms made a hole-in-one with a 5-wood in the third round of the 2001 PGA Championship. The course was originally designed by Robert Trent Jones, redesigned by George and Tom Fazio in preparation for the 1976 U.S. Open, and further redesigned by Rees Jones before the 2001 PGA.

No. 16 Oakland Hills Country Club
(South Course),
Bloomfield Hills, Michigan
ↄ
16th Hole, 406 Yards, Par 4

Classic courses of the 1910s and 1920s didn't often have water hazards pressed up against greens, but Oakland Hills is an exception. Donald Ross perched the 16th green behind a pond when the course opened in 1918, and it has been providing dramatic moments in major championships ever since. Cyril Walker clinched the 1924 U.S. Open with a bold shot that resulted in a birdie and Gary Player did the same with a 9-iron over a willow tree for a key birdie in the 1972 PGA Championship. A few contenders have seen their chances end with a splash on the 16th over the years, but the 2008 PGA Championship marked the first time the final-round leader made that cardinal error when Sergio Garcia let his approach slide to the right in an eventual defeat to Padraig Harrington.

The club has lost to disease the willow that Player hit over. In another change, Rees Jones extended the pond to bring it more in play on the tee shot—as if players didn't have enough to worry about.

No. 17 TPC Sawgrass (Stadium Course),
Ponte Vedra Beach, Florida
◯
17th Hole, 137 Yards, Par 3

There had been a few greens located on islands before. But when the TPC Sawgrass opened in 1981, its 17th hole became the first true island green, where the green itself formed virtually the entire island. Miss the green anywhere but a small pot bunker in front, and you're in the water.

That's the fatal attraction of this hole for resort golfers, who pump countless balls into the pond every year and keep coming back for more. It's also enough to give the pros white knuckles at the Players Championship, even though it is one of the shortest par 3s they play all year and requires only a 9-iron or wedge. This much-imitated hole actually came about somewhat by accident. So much earth around the proposed 17th green was dug out for use elsewhere on the course during construction that architect Pete Dye's wife, Alice, suggested filling the resulting hole with water and making it an island green.

No. 18 Doral Golf Resort & Spa (Blue Monster),
Miami, Florida
◯
18th Hole, 467 Yards, Par 4

This is once again the most feared finishing hole on the PGA Tour after thirty yards were added in 2004 by pushing the tee back. It was a double whammy. First, the change restored the old landing area for tee shots as originally designed by Dick Wilson, with water very much in play on the left. Distance gains on Tour had enabled players to reach a wider portion of the fairway past the point where the pond guarding the left side makes a bend to the left. No more, except perhaps in downwind conditions. Second, it means a longer approach shot. The pond continues all the way down the left side, and also makes a bend to guard the front of the green. Perhaps not so scary for the pros with a short iron in their hands, it's a different story with a mid-iron.

In 2007, when it played into the wind for most of the WGC-CA Championship, Doral's 18th ranked as the toughest hole on the PGA Tour for the entire year with a 4.625 average.

STRATEGIC
HOLES

The most interesting holes are ones that make the player think by giving him choices about how to proceed. This Dream 18 is an exercise in strategy, the only problem being that with so much thought involved, you might end up with a headache by the end of the round. But you will have had plenty of fun along the way, because these holes are never boring.

There is more than one kind of strategy on a golf course, though most types involve some sort of risk-vs.-reward equation. In some cases the option is whether or not to hit a driver off the tee; other holes offer alternate routes to the green, perhaps even two distinct fairways. Some involve the temptation of reaching a par 5 in two shots or a par 4

in one; in other cases the reward is more subtle, such as a better angle to the green.

The options on a given hole may vary depending on the player. It's no easy feat for an architect to build in options both for the pro and the mid-handicapper on the same hole, but that's what these holes accomplish.

It's harder to build options into par-3 holes, so we have included only three of them. But it's quite a pair of par 3s on our back nine, with Augusta National's 12th and Cypress Point's 16th widely considered among the best holes in the world. Nor is New South Wales's 6th a slouch. By including the full complement of four par 5s, this Dream 18 comes out to a par of 73.

Left: **No.16 Cypress Point Club, Pebble Beach, California** ◗ 16th Hole, 231 Yards, Par 3 *See page 149 for description.*

	Par	Black	Blue	White	Gold	Red			Par	Black	Blue	White	Gold	Red
1 Somerset Hills 15	4	394	375	375	301	301	10 Royal County	4/5	477	477	457	435	435*
2 Desert Forest 7	5	534	534	520	466	466	Down 3						
3 National Golf Links 3	4	426	416	411	378	378	11 Kiawah Island	5	543	528	501	495	419
4 Barnbougle Dunes 15	4	353	353	322	229	229	(Ocean) 2						
5 Bethpage (Black) 5	4	478	451	423	401	401	12 Augusta	3	155	155	145	145	145
6 New South Wales 6	3	195	195	169	169	140	National 12						
7 Club zur Vahr 6	5	545	534	502	476	400	13 The Country Club	4	335	335	324	324	262
8 Kingsbarns 6	4	337	318	287	287	241	(Composite) 4						
9 Mid Ocean 5	4	433	402	402	373	327	14 Erin Hills 14	5	615	505	469	434	312
							15 Commonwealth 16	4	400	400	372	372	337
Out	37	3695	3578	3411	3080	2883	16 Cypress Point 16	3	231	231	219	208	208
							17 Crystal Downs 5	4	353	353	345	345	244
							18 Muirfield 18	4	449	414	414	383	383
							In	36/37	3558	3398	3246	3141	2745
							TOTAL	73/74	7253	6976	6657	6221	5628

*Par five for women

No. 1 Somerset Hills Country Club, Bernardsville, New Jersey

ↄ

15th Hole, 394 Yards, Par 4

If you want to hit a driver on this hole, you had better hit a fade, because the fairway turns to the right before it reaches the point where a drive would come to rest for most players. The risk is going through the fairway or, conversely, having your fade turn into a slice and end up in the trees on the right side. The reward is a good birdie chance with a wedge to a green guarded by a picturesque stream.

The safer play off the tee is a 3-wood or long iron, but then you will be hitting a mid-iron second shot, which will make that stream to the front and left of the green look more dangerous. This was one of A. W. Tillinghast's early designs, the course opening in 1917, and one of his most charming.

No. 2 Desert Forest Golf Club,
Carefree, Arizona
⌒
7th Hole, 534 Yards, Par 5

Desert Forest opened in 1962 north of Scottsdale, designed by the unheralded Red Lawrence. The private club has no fairway bunkers per se, though it does have sand in the form of desert, and is a favorite of golf architecture aficionados. The strategic 7th hole is a good example of why.

From the tee, a player has a choice of shooting at either of two fairways. To play the hole as a three-shot par 5, the more accessible left fairway is used. But if a player wants to set up a chance to reach the green in two and has the length to make a desert carry, he can shoot at the right fairway. That more direct route to the green shortens the hole and enables a carry over a desert wash on the second. The safe route requires a layup short of the wash into the alternate fairway.

No. 3 National Golf Links,
Southampton, New York
⌒
3rd Hole, 426 Yards, Par 4

The expert golfer faces a choice of whether to hit a driver to a narrower part of the fairway, but it is the average player who really has a wide variety of options on how to play this hole. Called the Alps hole, patterned after the 17th at Prestwick in Scotland, it's a blind shot over a hill from the drive's landing area to the green.

It's a long hole for the mid-handicapper at 411 yards from the middle tee, so designer C. B. Macdonald extended the fairway so that the short hitter or a player who has not hit a good drive can take the straight route on the second shot and then pitch over the hill to his left on the third shot. Or he could lay up onto the higher plateau short of a bunker that crosses the fairway twenty yards short of the green. There is just enough room between that bunker and the green so that a player straining to reach the putting surface with his second shot can bounce his ball onto the green if he wants to take the bold route.

No. 4 Barnbougle Dunes, Bridport, Tasmania, Australia

15th Hole, 353 Yards, Par 4

The choice off the tee here is posed by a bunker in the center of the fairway. If you play your tee shot safely to the wider portion of fairway to the left of the bunker, you are faced with an angled approach to a green that drops off sharply to the left side—the side you are coming in from. A riskier drive to the right side of the fairway leaves a more favorable straight-on approach.

If you *really* want to be safe on the tee shot on this hole designed by Tom Doak, you can stay short of the bunker. Or, if you want to be bold, you can try to carry it, which requires flying the ball 256 yards from the back tee. But you won't have the luxury of a wide fairway, because a large bunker eats into the left side.

**No. 5 Bethpage State Park
(Black Course),
Farmingdale, New York**

⌒

5th Hole, 478 Yards, Par 4

The diagonal carry over a vast fairway bunker on the right side makes this a strategic gem from A. W. Tillinghast. Thanks to a new championship tee that brings the bunker into play for the pros, competitors at the 2009 U.S. Open faced similar choices to those faced by everyday players, unlike in the 2002 Open, when they were able to fly past the bunker.

The dilemma is how much of the bunker to try to cut off. If you try to make a longer carry, you will have a shorter second shot and a clear view of the green. But if you let the shot leak just slightly to the right, you will be in the bunker and probably unable to reach the green, because it is a long, uphill shot. If you play safely to the left to take the bunker out of play, not only will you face a longer second shot, you might end up blocked by trees from even shooting at the green. On such a difficult hole, it's truly a case of picking your poison.

No. 6 New South Wales Golf Club, La Perouse, Australia

◯

6th Hole, 195 Yards, Par 3

Alister MacKenzie designed New South Wales during a short visit to Australia in 1926, but left Eric Apperly, a fine local player, to handle the details, including all the bunkering. Apperly went further than that. During the 1930s, he added an entirely new hole, the 6th, requiring the building of a short bridge to a championship tee located on an island in the Pacific Ocean.

It has become the most photographed hole in Australia because of its spectacular setting, but the hole's playing values are more subtle. The presence of the ocean on the left causes a tendency to steer toward the right. But the green slopes severely right-to-left, so it is a tough up-and-down if you miss on that side, and a slippery downhill putt if you hit the green. In fact, there is a considerable buffer between the green and the water on the front and left, so playing toward the left of the green is a smart move.

No. 7 Club zur Vahr, Garlstedt, Germany

◯

6th Hole, 545 Yards, Par 5

This hole is unusual in that there is a row of trees running right down the middle on the second shot, with dual fairways to the left and right of it. There is also a stream cutting across the fairway at about 290 yards from the tee on the hole designed by German architect Bernhard von Limberger in 1970.

You need to be on the right of the fairway on the tee shot to be able to access the right fairway, and that requires a fade around trees off the tee (with less than a driver for a long hitter). The reward is a corridor directly toward the green and a chance to reach in two or lay up into a fairly narrow fairway where you are less likely to need to carry a front greenside bunker on your third shot. The hole plays as a conventional three-shot par 5 from the left side, with the trees blocking the way to the green on the second shot.

No. 8 Kingsbarns Golf Links, Kingsbarns, Scotland

6th Hole, 337 Yards, Par 4

There are at least three ways to play this Kyle Phillips–designed hole, depending on how long you hit the ball off the tee and what kinds of chances you want to take. The first is to hit less than a driver from the tee toward the low part of the fairway, leaving a blind second shot of about 120 yards.

There's also a "high road" to a plateau fairway to the right, but to get there you will have to carry a hillside with a bunker set into it. Long and medium hitters will have a choice of what club to hit, depending on how far they want to leave themselves from the green. *Really* long hitters can take the gamble of going for the green, utilizing a right-to-left slope from the plateau fairway toward the putting surface, but they will have to find a narrow entrance. A pot bunker awaits to the right of the green, rough-covered dunes to the left.

No. 9 Mid Ocean Club, Tucker's Town, Bermuda

ↄ

5th Hole, 433 Yards, Par 4

C. B. Macdonald, a pioneer of American golf architecture, used copies of Scottish holes, such as the Road hole at St. Andrews, as a feature of his courses. But he also came up with an original hole that has been much copied by other architects. It's the Cape hole, and the best example is the 5th at Mid Ocean.

A Cape hole confronts the golfer with a water hazard to be carried on the tee shot, with the hole playing as a dogleg so that a greater carry distance over water on the drive will result in a shorter approach shot. A safe, shorter carry will result in a longer approach. At Mid Ocean, the effect is heightened by an elevated tee that gives the player a great view of Mangrove Lake and the hole stretching out below. Also, the difficulty of a second shot to a narrow green flanked by deep bunkers makes it more rewarding to have a shorter second shot.

No. 10 Royal County Down Golf Club, Newcastle, Northern Ireland

ɔ

3rd Hole, 477 Yards, Par 4

The two main strategic features here are a ridge that cuts into the right side of the fairway past the drive zone and a fairway bunker in the drive zone on the left. The ridge means that a drive to the right side of the fairway will leave a blind second shot. A drive down the left side will give you a view of the green, but you can only get there if you have the length to carry the fairway bunker. Also, it leaves you a longer second shot, so even a long hitter might try to hit it down the right side, especially since there is a very tall directional marker behind the green to help you aim your second shot.

Of course, if you want to give yourself the biggest margin for error in avoiding Royal County Down's nasty rough, you might simply aim down the center. From there, you will probably be able to see the flagstick on your second shot, but not the green. This hole was the work of George Combe, a club member who made extensive modifications to the original Old Tom Morris course in the first decade of the twentieth century.

No. 11 Kiawah Island Golf Resort (Ocean Course), Kiawah Island, South Carolina

ɔ

2nd Hole, 543 Yards, Par 5

There's marsh, marsh everywhere on this Pete Dye–designed hole. Choices, choices everywhere, too. Off the tee, the player who wants to get home in two can gain some distance by flirting with the marsh on the left side. But it's the second shot where decision-making kicks into high gear. The marsh crosses the fairway about 210 yards from the green and then again at about 120 yards. Assuming a decent drive enables you to make the first marsh carry, there are three options. (1) Lay up short of the second marsh. (2) Carry the second marsh and leave a wedge into the green. (3) If you have hit a long drive, go for the green in two.

The last option is fraught with danger, as the green is elevated, narrow, set at an angle, and surrounded by waste bunkers and marsh. But Dye has given the long hitter the advantage of a layup area of his own: The best angle for a third shot is from a strip of fairway extending from the left front of the green.

No. 12 Augusta National Golf Club, Augusta, Georgia

◯

12th Hole, 155 Yards, Par 3

Perhaps the best strategy here is a simple one—aim at the center of the green no matter where the hole is located. But it's a short enough hole that such a strategy doesn't seem very appealing, especially to a pro with a short iron in his hands. Of course, that's why we've seen a number of disasters on the 12th hole over the years at the Masters.

The genius of this hole, designed by Alister MacKenzie and club founder Bobby Jones, is that the green is on a diagonal, with Rae's Creek following that diagonal in front. So if you aim at a flag on the left, you need to take one club less than you would to the middle of the green, and if you aim at a flag on the right, you need to take one club more. The green is very shallow, so it is important to control your distance and commit to your line off the tee. Stray to the left of that line and you will be long; stray to the right and you will be short—and probably taking a penalty drop.

No. 13 The Country Club (Composite Course), Brookline, Massachusetts

⌒

4th Hole, 335 Yards, Par 4

This hole looks like a dogleg from the tee because the fairway bends to the right around some bunkers and back to the left toward the green. You almost get the feeling that the green is tucked into a corner, but actually there is nothing to block the long-hitting player from having a go straight at the green from the tee. In fact, it's more reachable than you might think, because the last thirty yards run downhill. But there are a couple of things to give the long hitter pause. First, you can't see the green from the tee because of that downhill slope. Second, the green is very small, a more fitting target for a wedge shot than a driver, and the right front entry is guarded by a bunker.

If you get into trouble, you can't even blame a single architect. While the course dates from 1893, this is one of several holes that members added around 1906. In a redesign before the 1988 U.S. Open, Rees Jones built a new tee and reduced the size of the green to 3,200 feet.

No. 14 Erin Hills Golf Course, Hartford, Wisconsin

ɔ

14th Hole, 615 Yards, Par 5

Erin Hills is a public course that opened in 2006 and has already been selected to host the 2011 U.S. Amateur. Many feel it is on the fast track to being named a U.S. Open site. It's a big, bold design (by Michael Hurdzan and Dana Fry, in collaboration with Ron Whitten) in a very natural setting. The 14th hole embodies those attributes.

The fairway bends to the left around a fescue-covered hill. But long hitters can take a direct route over the "Sea of Fescue," shortening the distance to the green and either getting there in two or reaching the fairway just short of the putting surface. A choice is also posed by a bunker in the center of the fairway; the narrower route to the right of it shortens the hole a bit more. Of course, the 14th can be played as a three-shot hole by going to the left around the hill. It is designed so that it can play differently from day to day in a tournament, with three championship tees at 650, 615, and 588 yards. At 505 yards from the low-handicapper tees and 469 from the mid-handicapper markers, it is designed to give options to all levels of players.

No. 15 Commonwealth Golf Club, South Oakleigh, Victoria, Australia

◯

16th Hole, 400 Yards, Par 4

Two hazards define this hole, and skirting one means dealing more directly with the other. First, there is a pond on the left side of the fairway. The tendency might be to steer away from the water, but that leaves an approach shot that must carry a very deep bunker on the right side of the green. There is also the problem of stopping your approach shot on a green that slopes right to left. An approach from the left side of the fairway leaves a much better angle, but if you go too far left on the tee shot, you're taking a penalty drop.

Commonwealth moved its course from the clay-based environs of Melbourne out to the Sandbelt in the early 1920s, with an in-house design by professional Sam Bennett and club captain Charles Lane that has stood the test of time.

No. 16 Cypress Point Club, Pebble Beach, California

◯

16th Hole, 231 Yards, Par 3

A par 3 where one of the options is to aim somewhere else besides the green? It works at Cypress Point's 16th, owing to the magnificence of its setting and the spine-tingling drama of going for the green over some 200 yards of ocean. Designer Alister MacKenzie thought of making this a par 4 from a slightly longer tee, but club founder Marion Hollins, one of the top woman amateurs of her day, insisted that it was playable as a par 3. Time has proved her right, as many consider it one of the best holes in the world.

The alternate route is a mid-iron to a left fairway accessible via a shorter carry, and then a wedge to the green. Short hitters will take that route and long hitters will naturally go for the green, but the length of the hole is perfect for creating a dilemma for the majority in the middle. The prudent play for many would be to play it safe, but the daring play over the water is just too tempting.

See page 136 for photo.

No. 17 Crystal Downs Country Club, Frankfort, Michigan

○

5th Hole, 353 Yards, Par 4

Designer Alister MacKenzie masterfully used the undulations of this hole to create alternate routes off the tee. There's a lower fairway to the left and a higher fairway to the right, divided by the "Three Sisters" bunkers. A straight line from tee to green goes over those bunkers, then over a large bunker set into a ridge just in front of the putting surface (just the top of the flag is visible from the elevated tee).

The straight path is probably the least used because distance control must be precise to fit into the fairway between the Three Sisters and the ridge ahead of it. The route to the right leaves an easier second shot because the green—the work of co-designer Perry Maxwell—slopes from left to right. But it is a longer carry to that fairway, with a tree to fly over along the way and out of bounds to the right. The left route is safer, but leaves a blind shot that is more difficult to hold on a green that slopes down to four bunkers on the right.

No. 18 Muirfield
(Honourable Company of Edinbugh Golfers),
Gullane, Scotland

◯

18th Hole, 449 Yards, Par 4

The dilemma for the pro or long-hitting amateur here is whether to hit a driver off the tee and risk going into the fairway bunkers or to hit an iron and settle for a long approach into a green that is no easy target. The fairway bunkers are deep pits from which it is impossible to reach the green. Among the players who may have regretted using a driver are Paul Azinger, who lost the 1987 British Open by one stroke when he bogeyed after a tee shot into a bunker, and Thomas Levet, who bogeyed the 18th in both a four-hole playoff and the sudden-death playoff that followed to lose to Ernie Els.

Els at the 2002 Open represented the other strategy, using an iron all three times he played it in a tense Sunday. He scored three pars, but showed that laying up off the tee is not a foolproof method as his sudden-death approach shot found a greenside bunker. Still, he was able to get up and down to win the title. Originally designed by Old Tom Morris in 1891, Muirfield was considerably altered by Harry Colt in the 1920s.

WELL-BUNKERED

HOLES

The first bunkers on Scottish links courses were natural hollows dug out by sheep sheltering themselves from the wind. Once golf courses came to be purposefully designed, man-made bunkers became one of the main tools of the golf architecture trade.

Golf designers can put bunkers anywhere they want, and for a variety of purposes. Bunkers can be aesthetic, penal, strategic, or some combination of the three (steering clear of penal bunkers is a good strategy indeed).

Bunkers are places to avoid, but a clever architect can place them in such a manner that a player who is bold enough to flirt with a fairway bunker is rewarded with a better angle. They can also be placed to reward the player who is bold enough, or long enough, to carry over them.

The invention of the sand wedge in the 1930s and the firm sand found in present-day bunkers has taken some of the fear out of bunkers, which generally are not the places of punishment they once were. There are exceptions, however, and many of them can be found on this Dream 18.

Left: **No. 17 Bethpage State Park (Black Course), Farmingdale, New York** ↻ 4th Hole, 517 Yards, Par 5 *See page 167 for description.*

	Par	Black	Blue	White	Gold	Red
1 Pacific Dunes 8	4	400	400	369	349	296
2 Royal Liverpool 2	4	371	371	357	357	334
3 Oakmont 3	4	428	390	378	339	339
4 Royal Melbourne (East) 17	5	558	558	518	518	470
5 Hirono 5	3	152	152	135	135	135
6 Tullymore 6	4	378	337	331	286	241
7 Pine Valley 7	5	636	573	573	538	538
8 Woodhall Spa (Hotchkin) 5	3	148	148	143	114	114
9 Ganton 7	4	432	432	432	414	414
Out	36	3503	3361	3236	3040	2881

	Par	Black	Blue	White	Gold	Red
10 Whistling Straits (Straits) 11	5	619	552	516	504	468
11 Castle Pines 16	3	209	209	188	165	140
12 Sand Hills 4	4	485	449	409	409	307
13 Muirfield 13	3	191	191	146	134	134
14 Durban 3	5	515	515	508	508	454
15 St. Andrews (Old) 16	4	423	381	381	381	325
16 Riviera 16	3	166	166	148	148	125
17 Bethpage (Black) 4	5	517	517	461	438	438
18 Royal Lytham & St. Annes 17	4/5	467	432	413	404	404*
In	36/37	3592	3412	3170	3091	2795
TOTAL	72/73	7095	6773	6404	6131	5676

*Par five for women

No. 1 Pacific Dunes, Bandon, Oregon

○

8th Hole, 400 Yards, Par 4

A moderate-size, deep front bunker dominates the player's thinking on the approach shot here as it is in play no matter where the flagstick is located. The bunker doesn't prevent a run-up to either the left or right sides of the green, which remain open, but the shot must be accurate. The alert golfer— or one who has played the course several times—will note that there is a slope to the right of the green that kicks the ball back toward the putting surface, which can be useful if the flag is on the right. When the flag is on the left, avoidance of the highly visible front bunker may cause the player to flirt more than he needs to with a bunker on the back left.

The 8th is proof that there is much more to this Tom Doak–designed gem than the seaside holes and views. The inland holes are pretty special, too.

No. 2 Royal Liverpool Golf Club,
Hoylake, England
◠
2nd Hole, 371 Yards, Par 4

The best approach to the green is from the left side, because of the angle of the green and also because it's more open to come in from that side in terms of greenside bunkering. But there are bunkers on the left side of the fairway at 275 and 300 yards from the tee that must be challenged to put the ball in the best position.

The bunkers in front of the green are very deep and are to be avoided at all costs. When combined with the firmness of the greens that was demonstrated in the British Open's successful return to Royal Liverpool in 2006, it becomes a challenging approach even with a wedge or short iron.

No. 3 Oakmont Country Club,
Oakmont, Pennsylvania
◠
3rd Hole, 428 Yards, Par 4

Oakmont founder and course designer H. C. Fownes is famous for the dictum "A shot poorly played should be a shot irrevocably lost." He certainly employed that penal philosophy in building the course, and one of his diabolical inventions for doing so was the "Church Pews" bunker that divides the third and fourth fairways, coming into play on the left side of both holes.

The pews are a series of twelve grass-topped ridges within an extremely long bunker. The ridges ensure that even though the third hole is not a long par 4, it will be very difficult to reach the green from this bunker—impossible if the ball is at all close to a ridge. For good measure, there are five fairway bunkers on the right side, ensuring that this is a test of driving accuracy, and five more bunkers on either side of the green. But it's the Church Pews that most players will be praying to avoid.

No. 4 Royal Melbourne Golf Club (East Course), Black Rock, Victoria, Australia

◯

17th Hole, 558 Yards, Par 5

A diagonal line of five bunkers stretches from the left side of the fairway some fifty yards short of the green, across the fairway to the front right of the green. So in addition to the usual risk/reward scenarios of going for the green in two is added the possibility of carrying the bunkers on the left side of the fairway to leave an easier pitch into the green.

Royal Melbourne's East Course was designed by Alex Russell, a local protégé of architect Alister MacKenzie, who designed the West Course during a short visit to Australia. Russell's East Course meets those high standards and has six holes (including the 17th) that are used in the Composite Course for tournaments at Royal Melbourne.

No. 5 Hirono Golf Club, Kobe, Japan

⌒

5th Hole, 152 Yards, Par 3

English architect Charles Alison made a trip to Japan in 1930–31 and designed several courses. His deep, sprawling bunkers were so popular that bunkers in Japan came to be known as "Alisons." Alison designed Hirono, which is still hailed as Japan's best course and is known especially for its great par 3s.

The 5th hole is a beauty, playing over a water hazard surrounded by vegetation to a plateau green with a backdrop of trees. Three large, deep bunkers—left, right, and front—add to the aesthetic appeal, and also to the playing characteristics of the hole. This is a green you don't want to miss in any direction.

No. 6 Tullymore Golf Club, Stanwood, Michigan

⟳

6th Hole, 378 Yards, Par 4

Architect Jim Engh gave the bunkers at Tullymore a distinct look—many of them are long, narrow, squiggly, and marked by ridges along both sides. The bunker to the right of the 6th green, which starts well short of the putting surface, is one of those. But a small pot bunker in the middle of the fairway is an equally important element of the hole's design.

Long hitters may be able to carry the bunker to a wider part of the fairway, also affording a better angle to the green for their second shot. Others will face a choice of laying up short of the bunker or trying to fit their tee shot between the bunker and the marsh on the right. If they try the latter, a slice is disastrous.

No. 7 Pine Valley Golf Club, Pine Valley, New Jersey

ↄ

7th Hole, 636 Yards, Par 5

The central feature of the 7th at Pine Valley is "Hell's Half Acre," a vast sandy wasteland that actually measures more than an acre and needs to be carried on the second shot in order to get home in regulation. The bunker commences at about 275 yards from the regular tee and 340 yards from the championship tee and extends for 115 yards, covering the width of the fairway. This design by club founder George Crump means that the average player must hit a solid drive in the fairway to be able to carry the hazard and reach the green in regulation. A poor drive means laying up in front of Hell's Half Acre. For that matter, a poor second shot that doesn't clear the sand leaves a difficult third shot where the green is probably out of reach.

This had become a lay-up hole for long hitters until a new back tee was built in 2005 that added nearly sixty yards (at the same time, the regular tee was moved back about thirty yards to the old championship tee). Those few gorillas able to launch a 340-yard drive and contemplate going for the green in two would have to fly the bunkers that front the green, a 270-yard carry. For most players, those bunkers make for a challenging third (or fourth) shot to the green.

**No. 8 Woodhall Spa (Hotchkin Course),
Woodhall Spa, England**

ↄ

5th Hole, 148 Yards, Par 3

Woodhall Spa may have the deepest bunkers, as a group, of any course in the world. Most are larger than the pot bunkers found in Scotland, so you won't necessarily be up against the face, but that is of little consolation. The depth of the bunkers is primarily the work of S. V. Hotchkin, a member who leased some of his land to the club when it was looking for a new site, and eventually took responsibility for maintaining the course in the years after World War I. He did a lot of tinkering with the layout that was originally done by Harry Vardon and modified by Harry Colt, including digging the bunkers deeper virtually every year.

The 5th hole requires just a short iron, but the green is narrow and no easy target, especially in the wind. The bunkers are silent assassins, as they cannot be seen from the tee.

No. 9 Ganton Golf Club, Ganton, England

⌒

7th Hole, 432 Yards, Par 4

Bunkers have become decorative objects at many modern courses, but at Ganton they are deep and truly penal. You won't hear players rooting for an off-line shot to get in a bunker at this course that was originally designed in 1891 and has been reworked by a number of prominent architects since, including Alister MacKenzie and Harry Colt.

There are four bunkers at the inside of the dogleg at the left-to-right-bending 7th. They are no place to be, but if you are bold enough to steer your drive close to them, you will have a shorter approach shot and a better angle. The green is protected by two bunkers to the left and one to the right, with another in the fairway some seventy yards short of the green, just to throw off your depth perception.

No. 10 Whistling Straits (Straits Course), Haven, Wisconsin

⌒

11th Hole, 619 Yards, Par 5

A very long, very deep bunker extends from the left front of the green here all the way back down the left side of the fairway some 100 yards. The hole bends to the right and then a bit to the left, so the length of the bunker is on the line of flight for the rare player who has a chance to reach it in two. But Pete Dye has designed the hole so that the bunker is very much in play for others, too. Because the sand pit narrows the fairway and is so deep, the decision is whether to hit your second shot to the right of it and have a wedge into the green or play safely short of it and face an uphill shot of perhaps 130 yards. If you are unfortunate enough to find the bunker, you'll have to use the wooden stairs to climb in and out of it, except for the back portion.

No. 11 Castle Pines Golf Club, Castle Rock, Colorado

⟲

16th Hole, 209 Yards, Par 3

The bunker at the front left of the 16th at Castle Pines is very deep, but that's not the end of it. It's also a collection bunker that gathers balls from the front portion of the putting surface. If you're flying your tee shot over this bunker to the left side of the contoured green, you had better get it well over. What's more, this hole plays uphill, which makes the bunker look even more daunting from the tee. Of course, you can play toward the right side of the green, but what if you pull the shot? Then you're exactly where you didn't want to be.

This hole bedeviled PGA Tour players in the International, which was played at the Jack Nicklaus–designed course from 1986 through 2006.

No. 12 Sand Hills Golf Club, Mullen, Nebraska

⌒

4th Hole, 485 Yards, Par 4

There is only one greenside bunker on the 4th at Sand Hills, but it is one to remember. It's big, it's bold, and it's deep—some thirty feet deep, in fact. If you end up in there, you had better be able to hit a high bunker shot. The natural tendency is to steer toward the right, but there is a drop-off to the right of the green that makes getting up and down from that side no easy matter. With a long iron or fairway wood to the green, accuracy can't be ensured, so the bunker is more of a factor than it might be on a shorter hole.

While this bunker was dug out by designers Bill Coore and Ben Crenshaw, it has a natural, unkempt look, as do all the bunkers at Sand Hills.

No. 13 Muirfield
(Honourable Company of Edinburgh Golfers),
Gullane, Scotland
◯
13th Hole, 191 Yards, Par 3

Muirfield's bunkers are deep pits with steep stacked-sod faces—definitely places where you don't want to be. Unfortunately, the bunkers on the 13th are easy to find.

The green is narrow, so your tee shot doesn't have to be very far off to end up in one of the five bunkers (two on the left and three on the right).

The narrowness of the green also means that you might blast from a bunker on one side to a bunker on the other. That's just what Tony Jacklin did in the second round of the 1972 British Open, adding insult to injury by taking two shots to get out of the second bunker. He ended up losing by two strokes.

**No. 14 Durban Country Club,
Durban, South Africa**

ʒ

3rd Hole, 515 Yards, Par 5

This par 5 is like a bowling alley, with a row of bushes and out of bounds lining the right side and trees lining the left side. But it's a rumpled bowling alley, with the fairway dotted by humps, bumps, and hollows.

While there are only three bunkers, they are perfectly placed to add to the quality of the hole. There is a bunker on the left that eats into the fairway, practically halving its width at just the point a player needs to reach in order to have a chance to go for the green in two. Length must be combined with accuracy in order to get a two-putt birdie on this hole. For those who can't or choose not to go for the green in two, a pair of bunkers about fifty yards from the green, one on each side, keeps them on their toes.

**No. 15 St. Andrews Links (Old Course),
St. Andrews, Scotland**

◐

16th Hole, 423 Yards, Par 4

The bunkers at the Old Course all have names, and one of the most charming monikers is the Principal's Nose bunker that sits in the 16th fairway. There's nothing charming about the bunker itself. It sits smack in the middle of the double fairway for the parallel 16th and 3rd holes, forcing a player to drive to the right or left of it. Going right represents the shortest route to the 16th hole, but the drive must fit into a narrow area between the bunker and an out-of-bounds railway line to the right. Prudent players go left, especially since the length of the hole does not demand that the shortest route be taken. However, when coming into the green from the left, the Wig bunker must be carried.

No matter which path you take, the Principal's Nose itself is very much in play. It's a deep pot bunker from which you not only won't be able to reach the green, you might have to play out sideways.

No. 16 Riviera Country Club, Pacific Palisades, California

◯

16th Hole, 166 Yards, Par 3

Riviera's par-3 6th hole is known for having a bunker in the middle of the green. But the 16th, being on the back nine, gets more airtime during the PGA Tour's Northern Trust Open, and it's probably a better hole anyway. The bunkering here is just about opposite the 6th, as the green is positively ringed by traps.

It's a shortish par 3, but the bunkering is intimidating for the mid-handicapper and worrisome even for the Tour pro. The lips of the large bunkers at the front and front-right rise even higher than the surface of the green, which makes them impossible to ignore when you are standing on the tee.

No. 17 Bethpage State Park (Black Course), Farmingdale, New York

◯

4th Hole, 517 Yards, Par 5

No. 18 Royal Lytham & St. Annes, Lytham St. Annes, England

◯

17th Hole, 467 Yards, Par 4

A. W. Tillinghast employed big bunkers at Bethpage Black, and there are none more dramatic than the cross bunker set into a hillside on the 4th hole beyond the drive zone. It is huge, multifingered, and, because it is set in front of a higher tier of fairway, can be difficult to carry for the average player if he has hit a less than solid drive. The bunker is angled to the right, so that it will catch a faded shot that would otherwise have reached safety.

This bunker is not much in play for the pros, who can carry it even from the rough or the large bunker to the left of the fairway. But Tillinghast has sprung some traps for them, too. This is a par 5 that most pros have the length to reach in two, but with a large, steep-faced bunker in front of the green, the ball must be flown all the way to the putting surface. With an uphill shot and a green that falls away toward the back, it's very hard to stop the ball on the green. A better idea might be to hit the second shot out to the right, where Tillinghast has conveniently put the fairway in a place affording an easy pitch that doesn't have to carry the bunkers.

See page 152 for photo.

This hole is liberally sprinkled with bunkers, no fewer than twenty-one in all. Seven of them can be found to the left of the fairway to catch short, medium, and long drives that stray in that direction, the last two of them cutting into the fairway to narrow it. These bunkers have been placed there by various architects who have redesigned the course; when Lytham hosted its first British Open in 1926, this was just a vast, sandy area. The most important shot of that championship was a 175-yard recovery from that area by the winner, Bobby Jones, now marked by a plaque.

There is a break in the fairway, dotted with four bunkers, at about the point where the hole makes a turn to the left. The late dogleg means that most approach shots come into the green from the left side, and that's where four of the six remaining bunkers lie in wait.

BUNKERLESS
HOLES

Restraint can be a virtue in golf architecture. When a hole has interesting topography and other design elements going for it, there isn't always the need to dot the landscape with bunkers. In fact, there are some great holes that don't have a single bunker.

That includes the holes in this Dream 18, but this is not a definitive list of the best holes without a bunker. In fact, two of the most famous bunkerless holes appear in the Dream 18 on Links Holes, the 11th at Ballybunion's Old Course in Ireland and the 14th at Royal Dornoch in Scotland. A number of others are scattered through the book, including Hazeltine National's 16th, PGA West Stadium Course's 6th, and Royal Portrush Dunluce Course's 14th.

It is a bit surprising that links golf, so well known for its pot bunkers, has so many bunkerless holes. Links courses represented on this Dream 18 are Enniscrone, Ballybunion Old (the 6th hole instead of the 11th), and Royal Portrush Dunluce in Ireland; Royal Troon in Scotland; and Royal Liverpool in England. While not a seaside links, Royal Ashdown Forest's Old Course south of London goes the furthest—there are no bunkers at all on the layout.

The 6th hole at PGA West's Stadium Course uses water as a severely threatening hazard and the holes at Royal Liverpool and Wentworth prominently feature out of bounds. The other holes show that even with more subtle demands, bunkers are not always necessary.

Left: **No. 8 PGA West (Stadium Course), La Quinta, California** ↻ 17th Hole, 168 Yards, Par 3 *See page 175 for description.*

	Par	Black	Blue	White	Gold	Red		Par	Black	Blue	White	Gold	Red
1 Jockey Club (Red) 18	4	354	354	354	340	340	10 Ballybunion (Old) 6	4	382	382	344	324	285
2 Royal Liverpool 1	4	427	427	405	405	395	11 Royal Adelaide 3	4	293	293	288	288	272
3 Addington 12	5	485	485	459	459	429	12 Highlands Links 16	5	460	460	453	453	408
4 New South Wales 14	4	355	355	333	333	299	13 Mission Hills (Norman) 4	3	147	138	131	115	96
5 Fishers Island 4	4	397	397	355	323	317	14 Augusta National 14	4	440	440	380	380	380
6 Royal Ashdown Forest (Old) 11	3	249	249	249	240	240	15 Royal Portrush (Dunluce) 5	4	411	411	379	369	335
7 Enniscrone 16	5	514	514	469	460	447	16 Paraparaumu Beach 16	3	138	138	138	130	124
8 PGA West (Stadium) 17	3	168	146	131	112	83	17 Wentworth (West) 17	5	610	566	549	486	486
9 Royal Troon (Old) 10	4	438	385	385	367	360	18 Inverness 7	4	481	453	434	362	358
Out	36	3387	3312	3140	3039	2910	**In**	36	3335	3281	3096	2907	2744
							TOTAL	72	6722	6593	6236	5946	5654

No. 1 The Jockey Club (Red Course), San Isidro, Argentina

⌒

18th Hole, 354 Yards, Par 4

Alister MacKenzie was a great admirer of the Old Course at St. Andrews. When called upon to design two golf courses for the Jockey Club (a sporting club that dates to 1882) in the late 1920s, he saw that the flat land was reminiscent of St. Andrews, minus the little humps, bumps, and swales featured on the landscape at the famed Scottish course.

So MacKenzie quickly went about constructing his own humps, bumps, and swales.

The 18th at the Red Course is based on the 18th at the Old Course. A par 4 of moderate length, it is wide open and has no bunkers. While offering a good birdie chance at the end of the round, its main complicating feature is a "Valley of Sin" on the front of the green, where if a rise is not carried, the shot will roll back down into the valley. Unlike the 18th at the Old Course, there are also drop-offs at the sides and back of the green.

No. 2 Royal Liverpool Golf Club, Hoylake, England

○

1st Hole, 427 Yards, Par 4

Who needs bunkers when you have a cop to enforce difficulty? The "cop" in question is a narrow man-made ridge, just three feet high, that separates the course from the practice area. Anything on the wrong side of the cop is out of bounds.

The first hole bends diabolically around the cop, with the boundary running along frightfully close to the fairway for the last 160 yards and continuing on that path just five yards to the right of the green. If you don't hit a long drive down the left side, you actually have to hit your second shot *over* the out-of-bounds area to shoot at the green. This makes it probably the most intimidating opening hole in golf, though it was played as the 3rd hole in the 2006 British Open.

No. 6 Royal Ashdown Forest Golf Club
(Old Course),
Forest Row, England

⌒

11th Hole, 249 Yards, Par 3

Not only is this a hole without a bunker, it is a *course* without a bunker. The original charter of the land says that there may be no man-made alterations or excavations, so the course, located south of London, was built without bunkers in 1888 and has remained that way.

The 11th hole plays over a valley marked by scrub brush at the bottom and covered with fescue on the slope back up toward the green. Overall, the hole plays downhill, but it is still a long shot that will require a driver for many players to reach the hogback green. While the course has three sets of tees, this hole plays at least 240 yards for all of them, including the forward tees. It is listed on the scorecard as a par 3 even for ladies.

No. 5 Fishers Island Club, Fishers Island, New York,

っ

4th Hole, 397 Yards, Par 4

Like his mentor, C.B. Macdonald, course architect Seth Raynor nearly always included a par four with a blind second shot in his designs. These holes aren't necessarily bunkerless, but that's the way it worked out at Fishers Island's "Alps" 4th hole.

This hole challenges the golfer with its terrain from the tee shot all the way through. First, the golfer must make a carry up to a fairway that is set at a higher level. Once that is successfully negotiated, the player takes aim at a tall directional marker located behind the green. That's all he can see, because a huge mound about 20 yards short of the green completely obscures the putting surface. If the drive is less than solid, the mound serves not only to block the player's view but also looms as a formidable obstacle to carry.

**No. 6 Royal Ashdown Forest Golf Club
(Old Course),
Forest Row, England**

11th Hole, 249 Yards, Par 3

Not only is this a hole without a bunker, it is a *course* without a bunker. The original charter of the land says that there may be no man-made alterations or excavations, so the course, located south of London, was built without bunkers in 1888 and has remained that way.

The 11th hole plays over a valley marked by scrub brush at the bottom and covered with fescue on the slope back up toward the green. Overall, the hole plays downhill, but it is still a long shot that will require a driver for many players to reach the hogback green. While the course has three sets of tees, this hole plays at least 240 yards for all of them, including the forward tees. It is listed on the scorecard as a par 3 even for ladies.

No. 2 Royal Liverpool Golf Club, Hoylake, England

↺

1st Hole, 427 Yards, Par 4

Who needs bunkers when you have a cop to enforce difficulty? The "cop" in question is a narrow man-made ridge, just three feet high, that separates the course from the practice area. Anything on the wrong side of the cop is out of bounds.

The first hole bends diabolically around the cop, with the boundary running along frightfully close to the fairway for the last 160 yards and continuing on that path just five yards to the right of the green. If you don't hit a long drive down the left side, you actually have to hit your second shot *over* the out-of-bounds area to shoot at the green. This makes it probably the most intimidating opening hole in golf, though it was played as the 3rd hole in the 2006 British Open.

No. 3 The Addington Golf Club, Croydon, England

◯

12th Hole, 485 Yards, Par 5

The Addington is close enough to London to let you see the skyline, but it's a world apart. The 12th hole tumbles along a wild part of the property, downhill and then uphill, bending around a series of mounds and humps. Unless you lay up at the top of the hill at about 200 yards from the tee, the tee shot is an adventure. There is a twenty-yard-deep, man-made plateau fairway cut into the side of the downhill slope, but the rest of the downslope is covered with rough, and if you are not lucky enough to find the plateau, it's potluck as to what kind of lie you end up with. It's possible to reach the green from the plateau; otherwise you'll need to play your layup out to the right to set up an uphill third shot.

The course was laid out in 1912 by club founder John Frederick Abercromby, who designed a few other courses while also refining Addington over the next two decades.

No. 4 New South Wales Golf Club, La Perouse, New South Wales, Australia

◯

14th Hole, 355 Yards, Par 4

The first task is to get your mind off the view, as this hole plays along the coastline and provides one of many spectacular vistas at Alister MacKenzie–designed New South Wales. The drive requires a short carry over a ravine to a fairway notable for a ridge at about the 200-yard mark. Since the fairway leading up to this ridge is not level, there is not much point in laying up, and most players will hit a driver to catch the downhill slope on the other side. A drive too far left will disappear amid thick bushes on the ocean side; too far right leaves a worse angle for the second shot.

The approach is with a short iron, but it's not an easy one to a cliff-top green. You don't want to go long or left, because the ball will roll down a hill, possibly into thick vegetation.

No. 7 Enniscrone Golf Club, Enniscrone, Ireland

ↄ

16th Hole, 514 Yards, Par 5

This is one of six new holes architect Donald Steel added in 1999, when the club was able to incorporate some neighboring dunes land into its layout. The 16th plays through a corridor of dunes all the way from tee to green, forming a gentle dogleg to the right. A key feature of the hole is a dune that juts out from the left about twenty yards short of the green, blocking the left front of the putting surface. To reach the green in two, a player must be able to fly over this dune or go through a narrow entrance to the right of it. Failure means a probable lost ball in the long marram grass covering the dune.

The green is very shallow, making it difficult to hold with a second shot—sometimes even with a third. A few yards behind the green is a drop-off into dense growth, which again is lost-ball territory.

No. 8 PGA West (Stadium Course), La Quinta, California

ↄ

17th Hole, 168 Yards, Par 3

Pete Dye doesn't like to repeat himself, but the owners of PGA West specifically asked him to design an island-green 17th at their Stadium Course that opened in 1986. He obliged, but with a few twists to distinguish it from the 17th at TPC Sawgrass that made its debut five years earlier.

He bulkheaded the green with rocks instead of railroad ties, giving it a different look that is appropriate for its desert setting. He made the hole about thirty yards longer, increasing the size of the green by half to make it a bigger target. And, unlike at the 17th at TPC Sawgrass, where there is a pot bunker, he did not put any sand.

See page 168 for photo.

No. 9 Royal Troon Golf Club (Old Course), Troon, Scotland

☽

10th Hole, 438 Yards, Par 4

This is one of those out-and-back Scottish layouts where the 10th hole represents the turn back to the clubhouse. That can be a forbidding moment at Troon, where the prevailing wind is in the player's face on the back nine. To make matters even more difficult, the back nine is considerably longer than the front.

The home nine starts with a hole of medium length, but one that is formidable into the teeth of a strong wind. That wind can blow an imprecise drive into gorse bushes to the right or a gulley to the left. The fairway is broken up by a group of small sandhills past the drive zone. There is a drop-off to the right of the green that makes recovery shots difficult. Chipping is not so difficult if you miss the green slightly to the left, where it is flat. But if you go farther left, you might wish there had been a bunker placed there to keep your shot from bouncing into the gorse.

**No. 10 Ballybunion Golf Club
(Old Course),
Ballybunion, Ireland**

↻

6th Hole, 382 Yards, Par 4

There is out of bounds to the right, which moves closer to the fairway the farther you go off the tee, so that taking a driver and trying to get near the green is a risky play. But the biggest difficulty on this hole is hitting the green. It's not a long approach shot unless you mishit your drive or are hitting into a gale, but the green has a spine down the middle and tends to repel shots to either side.

This is the hole at Ballybunion that brings you to the ocean for the first time, with the Atlantic serving as a backdrop once you make the left turn toward the green.

No. 11 Royal Adelaide,
Seaton, South Australia, Australia
◠
3rd Hole, 293 Yards, Par 4

No. 12 Highlands Links, Ingonish Beach,
Nova Scotia, Canada
◠
16th Hole, 460 Yards, Par 5

Alister MacKenzie gave the club plans for a redesign in 1926 in order to avoid railway crossings. Along with the alteration of a number of holes and the rebuilding of some greens, it called for two brand-new holes, the 3rd and 4th. Only the 3rd remains exactly as MacKenzie designed it, and it may be the best on the course.

Long hitters may be tempted to try to drive this green, but the first problem they face is that the putting surface is hidden from view at the end of a downhill slope. The green is tucked between a dune on the right and a small diagonal ridge on the left that narrows the entrance to the front of a green that is described as a leg-of-mutton shape. Those who go for the green instead of laying up sometimes find out that they have bitten off more than they can chew.

Highlands Links, designed by Canadian architect Stanley Thompson and opened in 1941, has one of the strongest groups of par 5s of any course in the world. The 16th is noteworthy for its terrain. It runs uphill to the highest point on the course, so it plays longer than the yardage, but there is much more to it than that.

The hole plays shorter down the right side of the fairway, but it's very bumpy on that side, so if a player wants a better chance of getting a level lie, it's better to go down the left. The obstacle on the second shot is a steep bank, covered with rough, about sixty yards short of the green. It must be carried to have a chance of reaching the green in two. For those laying up, you will have a view of the top of the flagstick from about 100 yards away, but it will be a blind approach from closer to the bank.

No. 13 Mission Hills Golf Club (Norman Course), Shenzhen, China

○

4th Hole, 147 Yards, Par 3

After the Communist Revolution, China didn't have any golf courses until 1984, but Mission Hills is trying to make up for lost time all by itself. The complex in the burgeoning city of Shenzhen has no fewer than twelve courses, making it the facility with the most holes in the world. The Norman Course, named for designer Greg, is one of the newer ones and a stern test in a beautiful setting.

That summation applies to the 4th hole, which plays from an elevated tee with scenery including a forested hill as a backdrop and a lake to the left. The green is very long, which means that attention must be paid to club selection, but also very narrow, which means the tee shot must be accurate. Shots to the left are penalized the most severely, plunging down a steep hillside into probable oblivion.

No. 14 Augusta National Golf Club, Augusta, Georgia

ↄ

14th Hole, 440 Yards, Par 4

While it's only a gentle dogleg, this is one hole at Augusta where a right-to-left tee shot really pays in order to turn the ball around a group of trees on the left side. Also, the fairway slopes left to right and a ball that lands with draw spin is less likely to roll down into the right rough.

This hole's main defense is its putting surface. On a course known for severe greens, the 14th is one of the toughest. There is a large hump near the front center of the green that complicates the approach shot. Less noticeable, but just as important because it affects putts on all parts of the green, is the fact that the entire green tilts significantly from left to right. Within the last decade, the club expanded and slightly flattened the back left of the green, adding a hole location that is very difficult to get close to.

**No. 15 Royal Portrush Golf Club (Dunluce Links),
Portrush, Northern Ireland**

⌒

5th Hole, 411 Yards, Par 4

This Harry Colt–designed hole bends to the right at about the 200-yard mark, the rest of the fairway hidden from the tee by a dune. The question is whether to cut off some of the dogleg by flying over the dune, and if so, how much. The answer depends on how long you hit the ball and how much of a chance you want to take. If you miss the fairway, you risk losing a ball in Portrush's thick rough, and your search will be made more difficult by the fact that you couldn't see the ball land.

The approach shot is to a two-tier green, with a large mound blocking the view from the right side. And what a view it is, once you get to where you can see it. The green is backed by the North Channel that divides Northern Ireland and Scotland, with the out-of-bounds beach directly behind it.

No. 16 Paraparaumu Beach Golf Club,
Paraparaumu Beach, New Zealand

○

16th Hole, 138 Yards, Par 3

This short par 3 is almost a copy of the Postage Stamp hole at Royal Troon, with one big difference—there are no bunkers. But pitch shots from the rough around this green are at least as challenging as bunker shots would be, especially from the hillside to the left of the green, where, with a downhill lie, it can be tough to keep the ball on the narrow putting surface. The area around the green drops off sharply on the other three sides.

Australian architect Alex Russell overhauled an existing course in 1948, utilizing the land to make a links-style course that has long been acknowledged as one of the best in the country.

No. 17 Wentworth Club (West Course),
Virginia Water, England

○

17th Hole, 610 Yards, Par 5

No fairway bunkers are needed to make this a tough driving hole. The Harry Colt design has out of bounds running all the way down the left side, and a fairway that slopes sharply from left to right in the landing zone for tee shots. So, in order to find the middle of the fairway, the player has to aim down the left side—close to the out of bounds. A drive that lands in the right side of the fairway will kick down into the rough.

Wentworth annually hosts the European Tour's PGA Championship. With the championship tee recently pushed back some forty yards, this hole is no longer in reach except perhaps for the longest hitters in the right conditions. It now takes a poke of about 340 yards to reach the corner of the dogleg and bring the green into view.

**No. 18 Inverness Club,
Toledo, Ohio**

○

7th Hole, 481 Yards, Par 4

Donald Ross added this hole on newly acquired property when he thoroughly redesigned Inverness in 1918. The only change it has needed since is lengthening, from 438 yards to 452 and then to 481, the latter stretching done in 1999. Moving the tees back has kept the creek to the right of the fairway in play on the drive. That creek, incidentally, crosses the fairway at about 240 yards from the championship tee and 195 from the members' tee.

The second shot plays uphill to a green that is difficult to putt or to chip to. It has such a severe back-to-front slope that downhill putts have been known to trickle off the green.

No. 1 Stowe Mountain Club, Stowe, Vermont

◯

5th Hole, 394 Yards, Par 4

Stowe Mountain Club, a Bob Cupp design that opened in 2007, plays across rugged terrain near the base of Mount Mansfield, with captivating views and challenging shots. The 5th has an uphill tee shot to one of the highest points on the course, followed by a downhill approach, but it's the steep slope lining the entire right side of the hole that is most worrisome to the player.

To the right of the fairway, a fescue-covered hill might stop the ball from rolling too far down, but it might also be lost in the long grass. The area to the right of the green is more forgiving, with two thoughtfully placed bunkers to catch an errant approach and keep it from plunging into oblivion. Just don't miss to the right of the bunkers.

MOUNTAIN
HOLES

Mountains make for great scenery, but they are also a serious challenge for golf course architects. Golf was not meant to be played on steep slopes, so trying to fit a course onto rugged, up-and-down terrain doesn't always work. That's why true mountain courses are relatively rare, and often a disappointment from a playing perspective.

But when it all clicks, mountain golf can be spectacular. This Dream 18 showcases the true spirit of golf in the mountains. The holes all incorporate significant elevation changes and other elements such as rock outcroppings or streams. Holes that play in a flat valley with mountain views were not considered.

One of the problems with laying out mountain courses is the fact that uphill holes tend to be unappealing. But the holes can't all be downhill; it must all balance out, since courses generally start and end in the same area. Clever architects can get around this to some extent by making the steepest climbs be from green to tee (especially in this era when most players ride a cart), and by building uphill/sidehill holes instead of taking on a big hill head-on.

This Dream 18 doesn't have the same considerations, so it is weighted toward downhill holes. Combined with the fact that many of the holes are located so high above sea level that the ball flies farther, the course plays shorter than the listed yardage. It's an adventure through the Rockies, Alps, Appalachians, Himalayas, and Cascades. And, yes, the vistas are stunning.

Left: **No. 11 Sugarloaf Golf Club, Carrabassett Valley, Maine** ↻ 11th Hole, 216 Yards, Par 3 *See page 195 for description.*

	Par	Black	Blue	White	Gold	Red			Par	Black	Blue	White	Gold	Red
1 Stowe Mountain 5	4	394	380	314	274	209		10 Castle Pines 10	4	521	496	467	432	397
2 Himalayan 5	5	550	535	535	500	500		11 Sugarloaf 11	3	216	190	166	150	150
3 Kananaskis (Mt. Kidd) 16	3	207	207	164	135	121		12 Homestead (Cascades) 12	4	476	435	435	435	365
4 Sanctuary 4	5	571	535	491	464	436		13 Cliffs at Glassy 13	3	159	159	142	118	93
5 Eichenheim 7	4	344	344	329	314	281		14 TPC Snoqualmie Ridge 14	4	448	441	410	310	278
6 Chateau Whistler 8	3	212	184	184	158	123		15 Ironbridge 13	5	621	600	535	492	450
7 Ekwanok 7	5	597	597	572	528	528		16 Cordillera (Summit) 16	3	206	198	172	155	107
8 Crans-sur-Sierre 7	4	333	333	308	288	260		17 Montreux 17	4	464	450	421	405	336
9 Fairmont Jasper Park 9	3	231	231	214	182	170		18 Wade Hampton 18	5	555	535	535	420	386
Out	36	3439	3346	3111	2843	2628		**In**	35	3666	3504	3283	2917	2562
								TOTAL	71	7105	6850	6394	5760	5190

No. 1 Stowe Mountain Club, Stowe, Vermont

○

5th Hole, 394 Yards, Par 4

Stowe Mountain Club, a Bob Cupp design that opened in 2007, plays across rugged terrain near the base of Mount Mansfield, with captivating views and challenging shots. The 5th has an uphill tee shot to one of the highest points on the course, followed by a downhill approach, but it's the steep slope lining the entire right side of the hole that is most worrisome to the player.

To the right of the fairway, a fescue-covered hill might stop the ball from rolling too far down, but it might also be lost in the long grass. The area to the right of the green is more forgiving, with two thoughtfully placed bunkers to catch an errant approach and keep it from plunging into oblivion. Just don't miss to the right of the bunkers.

No. 18 Inverness Club,
Toledo, Ohio

○

7th Hole, 481 Yards, Par 4

Donald Ross added this hole on newly acquired property when he thoroughly redesigned Inverness in 1918. The only change it has needed since is lengthening, from 438 yards to 452 and then to 481, the latter stretching done in 1999. Moving the tees back has kept the creek to the right of the fairway in play on the drive. That creek, incidentally, crosses the fairway at about 240 yards from the championship tee and 195 from the members' tee.

The second shot plays uphill to a green that is difficult to putt or to chip to. It has such a severe back-to-front slope that downhill putts have been known to trickle off the green.

No. 2 Himalayan Golf Course, Pokhara, Nepal

☾

5th Hole, 550 Yards, Par 5

Set near the city of Pokhara and with a view of the soaring peaks of the Annapurna range, Himalayan is a unique nine-hole course laid out in a river canyon by ex–British Army major R. B. Gurung in 1998. The 5th green has a unique setting on a natural island in the Bijaypur River, which runs through the course. You actually have to cross the river twice on this hole, first on the tee shot and then on the shot to the green.

There is some sixty yards of fairway on the island leading up to the green, though it starts out at a width of only five yards before widening to twenty yards. Most players will be well served by staying short of the river in two and then shooting for the green with their approach shot. Conditioning is far from immaculate here, but playing this hole and this Himalayan course is more about the experience than what score you shoot.

**No. 3 Kananaskis Country Golf Course
(Mount Kidd Course),
Kananaskis Village, Alberta, Canada**

◔

16th Hole, 207 Yards, Par 3

An elevation of nearly 5,000 feet translates to about a 10 percent gain in distance, a difference of one or two clubs on a hole of this length. With the guesswork about club selection, Robert Trent Jones, Jr., did the golfer no favors with his design on this hole. If you come up short, you will probably find one of the bunkers fronting the green. Go long, and you find yourself with a difficult downhill chip on a green that slopes from back to front. At least you can console yourself with a view of the rocky peaks framing the green.

No. 4 Sanctuary Golf Course, Sedalia, Colorado

⌒

4th Hole, 571 Yards, Par 5

While only twenty-five miles south of downtown Denver, Sanctuary Golf Course is truly a quiet sanctuary. Surrounded by more than 12,000 acres of open space, the course was built by RE/MAX real estate founder Dave Liniger primarily to host charitable tournaments, and hosts only a few thousand rounds a year (it is not open to the public, nor does it have a membership).

The 4th hole on the Jim Engh design curves to the right around a hill. It plays downhill, so long hitters have a chance to reach it in two—if they can get around or over the hill and steer their way between a couple of trees and several bunkers. For players who can't reach in two, or those who decide to lay up, a tree in the middle of the fairway about thirty yards short of the green makes things interesting.

**No. 5 Golf Eichenheim,
Kitzbühel, Austria**

↻

7th Hole, 344 Yards, Par 4

Golf Eichenheim opened in the mountain town of Kitzbühel in 2001 and was quickly acknowledged as the top course in Austria. The Kyle Phillips design masterfully traverses the up-and-down terrain and takes advantage of the scenery of the surrounding mountains, nowhere more adroitly than at the 7th hole.

This shortish par 4 takes a right turn to head toward a large peak looming behind the green. The hole traverses an uphill and sidehill slope, so that anything short of the green or to the right will be carried away from the putting surface. It's a tough pitch shot from short of the green, and if you go right you will be fortunate to catch a large bunker to the right front rather than rolling down the slope.

**No. 6 Fairmont Chateau Whistler Golf Club,
Whistler, British Columbia, Canada**

↻

8th Hole, 212 Yards, Par 3

The view of the mountains in the background is pleasing, but there is little comfort for the golfer when he turns his attention to the hole in front of him at this Robert Trent Jones, Jr., design. Immediately to the right of the green is a large rock outcropping. To the left is a pond that wraps around the left front of the green. Where can you miss with your long- to mid-iron and still be reasonably OK? Front right, perhaps. Long, but only if it's straight. Left, but only if you catch a lone bunker or your ball hangs up in the long grass on the bank of the pond. Right, but only if you get a great bounce off the rock outcropping. Little comfort indeed.

**No. 7 Ekwanok Country Club,
Manchester, Vermont**

◯

7th Hole, 597 Yards, Par 5

Ekwanok is a mountain course because of its setting in the Green Mountains of Vermont. The 7th is a mountain *hole* because of the presence of a veritable mountain, in golf terms, that stands between the tee and the green. This

obstacle rises at about 300 yards from the championship tee and falls again at about 370.

The strong player will be able to fly over the hill with his second shot, but the short hitter or a player who has not hit a good drive will find the same challenge as most players did when Walter Travis designed the course in 1900—finding the narrow fairway that runs along the top of the hill and then hitting a long third shot that probably won't reach the green.

No. 8 Golf Club Crans-sur-Sierre, Crans-sur-Sierre, Switzerland

○

7th Hole, 333 Yards, Par 4

The Swiss Alps provide a magnificent backdrop for the course that annually hosts the European Masters on the European Tour, a layout that dates to 1926 and was substantially redesigned by Seve Ballesteros in the 1990s. The 7th hole provides the players with an interesting decision. The fairway makes a ninety-degree turn to the right at about the 240-yard mark, turning uphill and also getting skinny as it proceeds to the green.

There are no trees to block the players from ignoring that safe route and shooting straight at the green with their tee shot. It's only a 272-yard carry to the front of the green if you cut the dogleg, but it's uphill and the entire route takes you over rough and a pair of greenside bunkers. With birdies not terribly hard to come by via the conventional route, players must weigh whether the chance for an eagle is worth the risk.

No. 9 Fairmont Jasper Park Golf Club,
Jasper, Alberta, Canada

◯

9th Hole, 231 Yards, Par 3

Originally nicknamed the Cleopatra hole because it resembled a woman's form, architect Stanley Thompson replaced two mounds about sixty yards short of the green with bunkers just after the course's 1925 opening. But the hole is still quite a sight, tumbling downhill and playing directly toward dramatic Pyramid Mountain.

There is a bunker in front of the green, but it is fifteen yards short of the putting surface, so the ball can be bounced on. The green is built up onto a plateau short of the bottom of the slope, so missing the green to the left, right, or long results in the ball rolling down and leaving a difficult pitch shot.

No. 10 Castle Pines Golf Club,
Castle Rock, Colorado

10th Hole, 521 Yards, Par 4

A 521-yard par 4 with water directly in front of the green? It's either the hardest hole in the world, or it's at altitude and plays downhill. Fortunately, it's the latter, but the 10th at Castle Pines is still a stern challenge. Designer Jack Nicklaus originally conceived of this hole as a par 5, but club owner Jack Vickers decided to change it to a par 4 and make the 17th a par 5 to create excitement near the finish in the PGA Tour's International tournament.

For most of its existence, the 10th played at 485 yards. Considering that the hole plunges downhill for its entire length (with the mountain Castle Rock in view from the tee) and is at an elevation of 6,000 feet, that meant twenty-first-century pros were often hitting short-iron approach shots. The championship tee has been moved back by thirty-six yards, but the International ceased to be played after 2006.

No. 11 Sugarloaf Golf Club,
Carrabassett Valley, Maine

◯

11th Hole, 216 Yards, Par 3

No. 12 The Homestead (Cascades Course),
Hot Springs, Virginia

◯

12th Hole, 476 Yards, Par 4

It's a long way down from this elevated tee—128 feet down to the green, to be precise. The view, naturally, is spectacular, with nothing but forested slopes behind the green at this Robert Trent Jones, Jr., design. Running across the fairway and then to the left of the green is the Carrabassett River. There is a large bunker to the right of the green, but that's a better place to miss than left.

As testimony to the number of balls hit into the water, farmers fifteen miles downstream often find golf balls in their fields in the spring. They have been carried down the river and then into the fields with ice overflows.

See page 184 for photo.

The mountains of Virginia are the setting for The Homestead resort and its Cascades Course, designed by William Flynn in 1923. The 12th hole tests both distance and accuracy, as it is a long par 4 cut through the woods with trees lining both sides. For good measure, there is a creek running down the left. The hole tumbles downhill as it curves to the left, but for most golfers two solid shots are needed to get home in regulation. If you hit a bad drive, you have to worry about cross bunkers about ninety yards short of the green.

No. 13 The Cliffs at Glassy, Landrum, South Carolina

◠

13th Hole, 159 Yards, Par 3

The Cliffs at Glassy is located on a 3,000-foot plateau on Glassy Mountain, and the 13th hole takes you to the very edge of that plateau. You can see for miles and miles from the green on this Tom Jackson–designed signature hole on the course that opened in 1993 and launched The Cliffs Communities, which now has eight courses spread among the mountains of North and South Carolina.

As for the hole itself, watch out for a raised bunker on the left front, large boulders to the right, and a contoured green that can make two-putting difficult.

No. 14 TPC Snoqualmie Ridge, Snoqualmie, Washington
↻
14th Hole, 448 Yards, Par 4

A canyon intrudes between the tee and the green on this Jack Nicklaus–designed hole, with multiple choices as to where to aim off the tee. The fairway runs at about a ninety-degree angle on the other side of the canyon with the green set on the left side, where the carry over the canyon is longest. The direct route to the green is only 293 yards from the championship tee, certainly within the range of some players, especially since there is an eighty-foot drop in elevation. But in addition to the danger of hooking one into the canyon, there is a fourteen-foot-deep bunker next to the green that is a place to avoid.

Moving to the right, there is about a 265-yard carry to an area of the fairway where you will have a flip wedge to the green. Farther right is a fairway bunker, and to the right of that it's a 220-yard carry to the right portion of the fairway and a longer approach shot (as yet another option, if you can make the carry over that bunker you'll have miles of fairway width). The option of playing around the canyon and avoiding the carry exists from the front three tees.

No. 15 Ironbridge Golf Club, Glenwood Springs, Colorado
↻
13th Hole, 621 Yards, Par 5

Ironbridge Golf Club climbs 495 feet in elevation from the clubhouse to the 12th tee and then begins its descent. The 13th is downhill, but not dramatically so. The drama on the Arthur Hills–designed hole is a canyon that cuts diagonally across the fairway. Many players will face a choice of whether to lay up short of the canyon and leave a 150- to 170-yard third shot, or go for the fairway on the other side. The longest of hitters will have their own decision to make on whether to challenge a large bunker and go for the green in two.

**No. 16 The Club at Cordillera (Summit Course),
Cordillera, Colorado**

⌒

16th Hole, 206 Yards, Par 3

At about 9,000 feet of elevation, the Summit Course is the highest of four courses at Cordillera, and one of the highest in the nation. The ball flies about 20 percent farther in the thin air, so you can take two clubs less than the yardage indicates on the 16th, maybe even three less since it plays downhill.

You'll be happy to be hitting a shorter club, because the green is a fairly small target with a very deep bunker etched into a steep drop-off on the right side. There's another deep bunker at the front right of the green on this Jack Nicklaus design that opened in 2001.

No. 17 Montreux Golf and Country Club, Reno, Nevada

⌒

17th Hole, 464 Yards, Par 4

A tee set 100 feet above the fairway gives you a beautiful view of the hole below and the snowcapped peaks beyond. The scenery is beautiful, but what is liable to catch your attention is Galena Creek, which runs down the left side of the fairway and then cuts across to run past the right of the green. It is most threatening on the tee shot, where it practically hugs the fairway to catch a slightly hooked shot on a hole where you want to hit a long drive.

The Jack Nicklaus–designed course opened in 1997 and annually hosts the PGA Tour's Reno Tahoe Open.

No. 18 Wade Hampton Golf Club,
Cashiers, North Carolina

☽

18th Hole, 555 Yards, Par 5

Chimney Top Mountain looms over the 18th tee of a course that since its 1987 opening has been widely ac-claimed as one of the best mountain layouts in the Unit-ed States. Accuracy is a must on this hole designed by Tom Fazio, with a string of eight bunkers along the right side of the fairway and a creek on the left. The creek turns to jut in front of the left side of the green, making it a risky shot for long hitters attempting to go for the green in two.

LINKS

HOLES

Golf evolved centuries ago in Scotland on linksland, so called because it serves as a link to the sea. As such, it is marked by sandy soil and dune formations, sometimes large, as on the links courses of Ireland, sometimes small, as at St. Andrews where an otherwise flat surface is covered with a profusion of humps and bumps.

In an era before the lawn mower, there were sheep to keep the grass low. They also tended to gather in depressions to stay out of the wind, deepening those depressions, which formed bunkers when sand blew into them. And there were no trees to get in the way of hitting a ball toward a distant hole.

As it grew more popular in the nineteenth century, the game began to be played on all sorts of landscapes. Still, links golf holds a certain charm. More than that, the links landscape is well suited to the strategic type of holes that make the game interesting. It is no coincidence that Alis-ter MacKenzie, designer of Augusta National and one of the greatest architects, considered the Old Course at St. Andrews his favorite. Links courses eventually came to be designed or redesigned, first by golf pros in the nineteenth century and then by golf architects in the twentieth. But the links terrain allows the design to flow from the natural features of the land.

Linksland does not exist at all meetings of sea and land. There are precious few true links courses in the United States—even coastal courses such as Pebble Beach and Kiawah Island's Ocean Course are built on different kinds of terrain. While parts of Long Island might qualify, as might specific locales in Australia and a few in other places, this Dream 18 strives for absolute authenticity, so is limited to the links of Scotland, England, and Ireland. That, after all, is where people go on pilgrimages to play links golf.

Left: **No. 11 Ballybunion Golf Club (Old Course), Ballybunion, Ireland** ↻ *11th Hole, 451 Yards, Par 4 See page 213 for description.*

	Par	Black	Blue	White	Gold	Red		Par	Black	Blue	White	Gold	Red
1 Machrihanish 1	4/5	436	436	428	428	422*	10 Royal St.	5	548	535	535	507	491
2 Cruden Bay 7	4	380	380	344	344	336	George's 14						
3 Doonbeg 9	3	175	175	157	124	114	11 Ballybunion	4	451	451	400	384	346
4 European Club 13	5	596	503	489	489	413	(Old) 11						
5 Lahinch 5	3	154	154	148	143	118	12 Royal Birkdale 12	3	183	181	181	159	145
6 Royal North Devon 6	4	406	406	396	396	376	13 North Berwick 13	4	388	388	362	334	334
7 County Sligo 17	4	455	423	423	375	375	14 St. Andrews	5	618	530	530	487	487
8 Royal Portrush	3	210	202	202	195	167	(Old) 14						
(Dunluce) 14							15 Portmarnock 14	4	411	411	387	375	375
9 Turnberry (Ailsa) 9	4	452	432	388	376	376	16 Waterville 17	3	194	168	153	153	124
							17 Prestwick 17	4	391	391	391	375	375
Out	34/35	3264	3111	2975	2869	2696	18 Royal Dornoch	4/5	445	445	439	401	401*
							(Champ.) 14						
							In	36/37	3629	3500	3378	3175	3078
							TOTAL	71/73	7123	6841	6593	6264	5949
							*Par five for women						

No. 1 Machrihanish Golf Club, Campbeltown, Scotland

○

1st Hole, 436 Yards, Par 4

Many courses ease you into the round with an undemanding tee shot on the 1st hole. Not Machrihanish. Most players don't mind, however. In fact, many consider this the best opening hole in golf. It's certainly a unique setting with the tee on a spit of land and the fairway set diagonally on the other side of a beach. The farther left you aim off the tee, the longer the carry over the beach and the shorter the second shot into the green.

The fact that the beach is in bounds serves to ease players' minds on the tee. It's like a huge bunker, though it is marked as a lateral hazard because at high tide your ball could end up in the water.

The course is far off the beaten path, on the Kintyre peninsula in the southwest of Scotland. It has had a number of designers through the years, but the 1st hole was created by Old Tom Morris in his 1879 expansion of the course to eighteen holes. He is to be credited for having the foresight to devise this hole at a time when carries over such large hazards were rare.

No. 2 Cruden Bay Golf Club,
Cruden Bay, Scotland

☾

7th Hole, 380 Yards, Par 4

No. 3 Doonbeg Golf Club,
Doonbeg, Ireland

☾

9th Hole, 175 Yards, Par 3

Some call it quirky, others a hidden masterpiece, but all agree it is worth the trek to northern Scotland to experience this adventure through the dunes. First laid out by Old Tom Morris in 1899, the course was considerably altered by Tom Simpson in 1926 and he is most responsible for what we see today.

The 7th hole features an uphill second shot to a small green framed on either side by large dunes at the entrance. The hole is a dogleg to the left, where players may be tempted to cut the corner if they have enough distance to carry three pot bunkers. Because of the difficulty of the second shot, having a shorter approach into the green is enough of an advantage to tempt some to take the gamble.

Greg Norman designed this modern links, which opened in 2002, and moved very little earth in doing so. He routed the 9th hole very close to the beach, which practically hugs the left side of the green. While Doonbeg generally has won rave reviews, the one reservation most often voiced is about its difficulty. This hole provides an example: There is an out-of-bounds fence very close on the left side, but the right side is guarded by a pair of deep bunkers and a tall dune covered with thick grass. The front part of the green is narrow; the back portion is wider but partially tucked behind the dune. Still, it's a very natural hole in a picturesque setting.

No. 4 The European Club, Brittas Bay, Ireland
↺
13th Hole, 596 Yards, Par 5

Course owner/architect/former golf writer Pat Ruddy describes the challenge of this hole as "being between the devil and the deep blue sea." The devil comes in the form of deep bunkers along the left side of the fairway. The deep blue sea is the Irish Sea to the right, close enough to be a threat and not just a pretty view (though it is that).

The championship tees at The European Club stretch to 7,325 yards, which means they are mainly for the ace player. This hole plays just 503 and 489 yards from the tees that get the most use, so the average player doesn't have to be too concerned with distance. He does need to be very concerned with accuracy, and also with the decision to be made on the second shot, where the hole bends to the left to start its run parallel to the beach. Players can try to cut the dogleg to get near or on the green in two, or play more safely down the fairway to set up a full third shot.

No. 5 Lahinch Golf Club, Lahinch, Ireland

⊃

5th Hole, 154 Yards, Par 3

It's not unusual on a links course for a green to be tucked in a depression among the dunes. It is unusual for such a green to be located directly *behind* a massive dune. But that's what you have at Lahinch's famous Dell hole, a par 3 where the green is totally hidden from view. The aiming point is a white stone on the tee side of the hill, which is moved each day to indicate the hole location. The green is shallow, with another tall dune behind it.

The hole was designed by Old Tom Morris in 1894, long before the term "signature hole" came into use. In effect, that's what it quickly became, and Alister MacKenzie left the Dell untouched when he redesigned the course in 1927.

No. 6 Royal North Devon Golf Club,
Westward Ho!, England

☽

6th Hole, 406 Yards, Par 4

When Old Tom Morris came down from Scotland to design England's first course, Royal North Devon, in 1864, he found linksland that must have reminded him of home. The wrinkled and hummocky 6th fairway looks much like those at St. Andrews, and the scattered bunkering is reminiscent of the Old Course. Two bunkers to the left are the dangers for shorter hitters, but three pits dug into the middle of the fairway farther along are even more treacherous. They come into play for long hitters, or for others when the hole is downwind. The green features a big drop-off to the right side.

There is one difference from St. Andrews. The hole plays directly along the coast, and the views are more magnificent than anything found at the Old Course.

No. 7 County Sligo Golf Club,
Rosses Point, Ireland

◠

17th Hole, 455 Yards, Par 4

There is no way around a difficult approach shot at this hole designed by Harry Colt when he redid the course in 1927 and expanded it to eighteen holes. The fairway ends abruptly at about 275 yards from the championship tee (about 245 yards from the regular tee), plunging into a deep hollow, so long hitters need to lay up. Short hitters, on the contrary, must hit a good drive just to have a chance of getting home in two.

The hole turns to the left to a green set among the dunes. The front part of the green slopes back down toward the fairway, so if you don't get your approach well onto the putting surface, it will roll back down into the "valley of sin" and you will be chipping instead of putting your next shot.

**No. 8 Royal Portrush Golf Club
(Dunluce Course),
Portrush, Northern Ireland**

☽

14th Hole, 210 Yards, Par 3

The club's course guide helpfully says "play to the left of the green." But just one look from the tee is enough for most golfers to draw the same conclusion. To the right of the green is a sixty-five-foot drop-off to a deep depression. It's not a sheer drop-off, so you might have a shot from near the top of it—if you can find your ball and have a decent lie in the long grass. But it's definitely a place to avoid (and, by the way, your tee shot has to carry across the depression, too, with the distance depending how far right or left you go, so be sure to hit it solid).

English architect Harry Colt designed the Dunluce Course in 1932 on new land the club had purchased to expand to thirty-six holes. His creation at the 14th was given the name "Calamity Corner," for good reason.

No. 9 Turnberry Resort (Ailsa Course), Turnberry, Scotland

9th Hole, 452 Yards, Par 4

After being largely paved over with runways and used as a Royal Air Force facility during World War II, Turnberry was given an entirely new course by architect Mackenzie Ross in 1949. Ross moved it to the sea so that he could incorporate the sand hills, and nowhere did he move it closer than at the 9th hole. A narrow pathway leads to the championship tee located on a small spit of land, with a carry of some 200 yards over the crashing surf to reach the fairway. It is one of the most thrilling tee shots in golf.

This hole is also noteworthy for its landmarks. It runs past the remains of Robert the Bruce's Castle and a landmark lighthouse, and features a view of the island Ailsa Craig in the distance. As for the hole itself, once you get past the tee shot, it is notable mostly for a hogback fairway that feeds slightly off-center shots to the right and left rough, and a typically rolling links green.

No. 10 Royal St. George's Golf Club, Sandwich, England

14th Hole, 548 Yards, Par 5

The first thing that catches the golfer's attention standing on the tee is the row of out-of-bounds stakes lining the right side, practically pressing up against the edge of the fairway. That's intimidating, especially for slicers. The next thing to notice is a water hazard, known as the Suez Canal, crossing the fairway at 328 yards from the championship tee. Given the firm conditions usually found at Royal St. George's, the hazard is within reach of many of the pros when they play in the British Open.

Before the 2003 Open, architect Donald Steel designed a new green forty-three yards behind the old one (the original layout of the course was by club founder Dr. Laidlaw Purves in 1887). He also moved the green closer to the out of bounds to make a player think long and hard before taking the gamble of going for the green in two. Shorter hitters have to decide how to play around a pair of bunkers in the middle of the fairway about sixty yards short of the green.

No. 11 Ballybunion Golf Club (Old Course),
Ballybunion, Ireland

◠

11th Hole, 451 Yards, Par 4

No. 12 Royal Birkdale Golf Club,
Southport, England

◠

12th Hole, 183 Yards, Par 3

Few places in the world are more inspiring to a golfer than the 11th tee at Ballybunion's Old Course. The sea and beach to the right and below, dunes to the left, and the fairway ahead tumbling downhill over bumpy ground to the distant green—a perfect combination of beauty and challenge.

It's pretty obvious that you don't want to hit your drive to the right here, but the left rough is no bargain, either. The entrance to the green is a narrow one between dunes, so if you're going to play a run-up shot after a bad drive, it needs to be accurate. There are no bunkers to be found, but with the green falling off on three sides a variety of challenging pitch shots await those who miss the green.

See page 202 for photo.

The championship version of Royal Birkdale dates to 1931 when Fred Hawtree and J. H. Taylor significantly remodeled the course. But the 12th hole dates only to the 1960s, when Fred Hawtree, Jr., made some further modifications. The hole was in his father's original plans, but not built at the time because the money ran out. It is such a worthy addition that many consider it the best hole on the course, and one of the best par 3s in Britain.

The green is set among sand hills that prevent the flag from blowing to indicate the direction of the wind that will affect the ball in the air. It's a narrow target, with small, deep bunkers at the front left and front right corners and a drop-off on the left side.

No. 13 North Berwick Golf Club, North Berwick, Scotland

◠

13th Hole, 388 Yards, Par 4

An old stone wall runs along the left side of the fairway here, which is pretty unusual. Then the wall cuts diagonally in front of the green and on past the right side of it, which is *very* unusual. What the hole loses by not allowing links-style run-up shots, it gains in links-style quirkiness. (The 13th hole was part of an extension to eighteen holes in 1877, with further refinement in 1895.)

While it's not a big deal for the expert golfer, the three-foot-high wall is definitely a factor for the mid-handicapper, who may face a mid-iron shot over the wall. The obstacle is just a few feet short of the green, and also comes into play on a pushed approach. A weak approach to the right could leave a pitch over the wall—or a big problem if the ball nestles close to the obstacle.

No. 14 St. Andrews Links (Old Course),
St. Andrews, Scotland
↻
14th Hole, 618 Yards, Par 5

The 14th hole at the centuries-old Old Course wasn't fashioned by a golf architect, but by locals hitting feathery golf balls over natural links terrain. But no architect could have come up with a better strategic hole. There are at least three different ways to play it. Depending on wind conditions and varying thought processes, the same golfer might play the hole three different ways in three rounds.

For some, the drive is a tight one between the Beardies bunkers on the left and the out-of-bounds stone wall on the right; for those who can fly it past the Beardies, it's a

relatively simple one to the Elysian Fields. Strategy comes into play on the second shot, thanks to the huge Hell bunker that sits on the direct route to the green, ending some eighty yards short of the putting surface. If you have the length and the moxie, you can try to carry the bunker. The timid can lay up short and right of it, also avoiding the Kitchen and Beaty bunkers. But an integral part of the Old Course design is that it has double fairways, and probably the most used option is to play to the left of Hell bunker into the 5th fairway.

Before the 2005 British Open, the championship tee was moved way back across the stone wall to the grounds of the adjacent Eden Course, an area that is otherwise out of bounds when playing the Old Course. This drastic measure was taken to bring the hole's most salient strategic feature, Hell bunker, back into play.

No. 15 Portmarnock Golf Club, Portmarnock, Ireland

◌

14th Hole, 411 Yards, Par 4

The great British golf writer Bernard Darwin once wrote, "I know of no greater finish in the world than that of the last five holes at Portmarnock." The 14th starts that stretch with a medium-length par 4 that requires accuracy off the tee to avoid a trio of deep bunkers to the left and another farther down on the right. The second shot to a plateau green is even more demanding, with two bunkers set into the hill in front. There's a little bit of leeway to bounce the ball onto the putting surface, but not much, and another bunker eats into the right side of the green.

Portmarnock was laid out in 1894 by Scotsmen W. C. Pickeman and George Ross. It is known as one of the toughest links courses in Ireland, but also one of the fairest.

No. 16 Waterville Golf Links, Waterville, Ireland

☽

17th Hole, 194 Yards, Par 3

The back tee on this hole is known as Mulcahy's Point, because it was the favorite spot of course founder John Mulcahy and where his ashes are buried. It rises some 250 feet above sea level, which is impressive considering that it is less than 100 yards from the beach. The tee is set on the highest dune on a course wonderfully crafted by Irish architect Eddie Hackett on the west coast of Ireland in 1973.

As you might expect, the view is spectacular. The hole itself is wonderful, too, playing to a diagonal green with a deep bunker set into a drop-off to the left. There is mounding to the right of the putting surface, and the beach farther right. Descending to the green is like going down a set of stairs, with each tee box set on top of its own dune.

No. 17 Prestwick Golf Club, Prestwick, Scotland

◯

17th Hole, 391 Yards, Par 4

There are two geographically named obstacles to cross on this hole, first the Alps and then the Sahara. Actually, the hole calls for you to fly over both of them on your second shot—if you can. Your drive, if it is a good one, will take you up to a plateau fairway, but then you have a huge hill ahead of you, which gives the hole its Alps moniker and means that you have no view of the green on your second shot. The hole plunges down on the other side of the hill to a green fronted by a huge, deep bunker—the Sahara.

Prestwick opened in 1851 as a twelve-hole course designed by Old Tom Morris. The course was considerably changed when it was expanded to eighteen holes in 1883, but the Alps remained close to the original. They knew better than to change a good thing.

MODERN

HOLES

The 1980s and 1990s were boom times for golf course construction, the greatest flurry of activity since the golden age of architecture in the 1920s. It was an era when golf architects gained higher profiles and came to be more closely identified with their courses than ever before. The Big Three of the era were Pete Dye, Jack Nicklaus, and Tom Fazio, all of whom are represented by multiple courses on this list.

Earthmoving had already been around for a while in golf course building, but it was raised to another level in this era. Two of the holes on this list are from courses that were created from basically nothing—Fazio's Shadow Creek in the Nevada desert and Robert Trent Jones, Jr.'s Chambers Bay in a Washington mining pit. The same can be said for Dye's Whistling Straits (represented on other Dream 18s)

and a number of other courses. Some courses, including Nicklaus's Old Works, were even built on toxic waste sites.

While all this manufacturing was going on, a recent "minimalist" movement was afoot to get back to more natural courses. These are represented on this list by Eddie Hackett's Carne in Ireland and David McLay Kidd's Bandon Dunes in Oregon, and on other Dream 18s by the works of Tom Doak and Ben Crenshsaw/Bill Coore. But such courses can be built only on terrain that is perfectly suited for golf, so pushing earth around still has its place.

The pace of new course building has slowed recently, especially in the United States. But golf continues to push into new frontiers—including Brazil with the spectacular Terravista and China with the twelve-course complex of Mission Hills.

Left: **No. 15 Black Diamond Ranch (Quarry Course), Lecanto, Florida** ↻ 15th Hole, 358 Yards, Par 4 *See page 234 for description.*

	Par	Black	Blue	White	Gold	Red		Par	Black	Blue	White	Gold	Red
1 Bigwin Island 6	4	462	441	412	412	356	10 Chambers Bay 2	4	404	395	366	337	301
2 Carne 17	4	439	439	431	381	374	11 Huntsville 2	4	391	363	329	321	301
3 Pumpkin Ridge	5	470	470	450	423	393	12 Valderrama 4	5	558	517	506	481	459
(Witch Hollow) 14							13 Terravista 14	3	216	161	161	128	107
4 Bandon Dunes 4	4	410	410	362	340	308	14 TPC Sawgrass	4	481	436	377	377	334
5 Loch Lomond 5	3	190	175	150	150	110	(Stadium) 14						
6 Old Works 6	5	600	570	552	497	459	15 Black Diamond	4	358	354	318	285	285
7 Giants Ridge	4	478	455	424	424	347	Ranch (Quarry) 15						
(Quarry) 8							16 Mission Hills	5	580	555	535	503	443
8 Shadow Creek 17	3	164	164	129	129	129	(Olazabal) 5						
9 Honors Course 9	4	369	355	340	330	280	17 Cabo del Sol	3	178	150	137	112	102
							(Ocean) 17						
Out	36	3582	3479	3250	3086	2756	18 Kiawah Island	4	439	421	396	386	314
							(Ocean) 18						
							In	36	3605	3352	3125	2930	2646
							TOTAL	**72**	**7187**	**6831**	**6375**	**6016**	**5402**

No. 1 Bigwin Island Golf Club,
Huntsville, Ontario, Canada
○
6th Hole, 462 Yards, Par 4

No. 2 Carne Golf Links,
Belmullet, Ireland
○
17th Hole, 439 Yards, Par 4

Bigwin Island in the Muskoka region of Ontario was a popular high-end resort in the 1920s and 1930s. But the hotel ultimately failed and a Stanley Thompson–designed golf course went to seed. Golf is back on Bigwin with a new course designed by Canadian architect Doug Carrick that opened in 2001.

The 6th hole provides a stunning view of Lake of Bays from its tee perched more than 100 feet above the fairway. You can get plenty of distance on your tee shot here, so the hole doesn't play as long as it appears on the scorecard. The best angle to approach the green is from the left side of the fairway, and that's the side where two bunkers await to catch errant tee shots. Bigwin Island is reachable by ferry from nearby Norway Point.

Carne Golf Links is laid out on dramatic dunes land perfect for golf, but was not built until 1992, when a tourism company in this remote part of northwestern Ireland decided that a golf course was a good way to attract visitors. It was Irish architect Eddie Hackett's last course, a project he enthusiastically took on at the age of seventy-seven. It's a very natural course that needed only eighteen bunkers.

The 17th is the toughest hole at Carne. It plays long because it is uphill, but has a fairway that narrows between a depression on the left and a tall dune on the right just where the long hitters can reach with their drive. The green is long and narrow, this time with a dune on the left and a depression on the right.

**No. 18 Royal Dornoch Golf Club
(Championship Course), Dornoch, Scotland**

◯

14th Hole, 445 Yards, Par 4

Golf has been played at northern Scotland's Royal Dornoch for centuries, but the course as it exists today was designed by Old Tom Morris in 1877. There have been alterations over the years, but none to the 14th hole. It's hard to see what could be changed, since the hole is completely natural and its challenge springs from the contours of the existing land, with not a single bunker.

The hole follows a path traced by a dune line along the right side, which makes it somewhat of a double dogleg, turning to the left after the drive but to the right in the last twenty yards or so. Originally, it took players three shots to reach this green, but it now plays as a par 4, with a draw the best play off the tee, followed by a fade into the green. (Less accomplished players may still need three shots to get home, since it plays a stout 439 yards from the regular tees.)

The genius of the hole is the site of the green, which sits on a natural plateau five to ten feet above the fairway. The rise is largest on the right side, but the green narrows on the left and is a difficult target because it falls off on the left and rear. This is where the great architect Donald Ross grew up, and he learned his lessons well.

No. 3 Pumpkin Ridge Golf Club (Witch Hollow Course), North Plains, Oregon

14th Hole, 470 Yards, Par 5

It says par 5 on the scorecard, but for the better player this is a par 4 1/2. A pond guards the left front of the green, but if you can drive it far enough to have an iron into the green, it's probably worth taking a chance. If you need a full-blooded 3-wood to get there, it's probably better to lay up. You can run the ball up to the right side of the green, but it's such a narrow area between the water to the left and a bunker to the right that it's probably not a wise move.

The Bob Cupp design opened in 1992 and has hosted the 1996 U.S. Amateur and 1997 and 2003 U.S. Women's Opens. In 2003, the 14th was played as a 393-yard par 4 for the women, and was the toughest hole on the course. You can call the 14th a tough par 4 or an easy par 5, but it's probably better just to call it a very good hole.

No. 4 Bandon Dunes, Bandon, Oregon
◠
4th Hole, 410 Yards, Par 4

No. 5 Loch Lomond Golf Club, Luss, Scotland
◠
5th Hole, 190 Yards, Par 3

The original course at Bandon Dunes Resort, which created a splash when it opened in 1999, has been somewhat overshadowed since the arrival of its sister course, Pacific Dunes. But the Bandon Dunes course, by Scottish architect David McLay Kidd, is still worthy of praise both for its design and its beautiful setting.

The oceanside location provides a postcard moment at the 4th hole, which is the first time the Pacific comes into view. It is not in sight for the drive, which is a difficult one to a fairway bordered by long grasses on either side. But then the hole makes a turn to the right, becomes more open, and the magnificent Pacific backdrop is revealed. The second shot is not quite as challenging, though care should be taken to avoid a pair of bunkers on the left side.

This is the most beautiful spot on a course known for its beauty, playing directly toward Loch Lomond. But there is more to this hole than a scenic backdrop. A ridge runs through the middle of the long but narrow green, so you'll want to get your tee shot on the proper side of it. The cardinal sin on this hole is to hit it into the long bunker flanking the left of the green; it's a very tough up and down from there.

American architects Tom Weiskopf and Jay Morrish fashioned a very American course at Loch Lomond, but that was appropriate given that the turf is softer than fast-running linksland. Many consider it to be the best inland course in Scotland.

No. 6 Old Works Golf Course,
Anaconda, Montana

☽

6th Hole, 600 Yards, Par 5

This land, formerly used for copper smelting, was an Environmental Protection Agency Superfund site before someone had the bright idea to build a golf course. It required an engineered soil cover some eighteen to twenty-three inches thick over the entire site in order to

cap the waste material. The Jack Nicklaus–designed course embraces its history and has bunkers filled with black slag, giving the layout a distinctive look.

The 6th hole plays through two large slag piles, giving it the name Black Canyon. There's also a huge bunker on the left that comes into play on both the second and third shots. You especially want to avoid it on the approach shot, because at the green the bunker is ten feet deep and if you're not a good bunker player, you may be covered with black slag before you get out.

No. 7 Giants Ridge Golf & Ski Resort (Quarry Course), Biwabik, Minnesota

◯

8th Hole, 478 Yards, Par 4

Jeffrey Brauer's second course at Giants Ridge, which opened in 2003, was built specifically to challenge the low-handicapper. It does that, but he also made it playable for the average golfer from the middle tees. The 8th hole provides an example. It's tough because it's long, and it has strategic interest for the better player in the form of a large diagonal waste bunker on the right side. Bite off more of the bunker and the reward is a better view and slightly shorter approach shot. It's a deep bunker, though, so if you hit into it, reaching the green in two is unlikely.

The second shot is uphill, but the green complex is not too severe. You can run your approach onto the green if you are accurate enough to hit it at the left half of the putting surface; on the right side, a slope tends to feed the ball away from the green and toward a chipping area.

No. 8 Shadow Creek,
North Las Vegas, Nevada
○
17th Hole, 164 Yards, Par 3

Shadow Creek is a verdant wonderland in the desert north of Las Vegas, complete with thick stands of pine and cottonwood trees, gurgling streams, a rolling landscape, and even exotic birdlife. Of course, this was a piece of dead-flat desert property before Vegas mogul Steve Wynn and golf architect Tom Fazio got hold of it in the late 1980s (the course opened in 1989). They spent an estimated $46 million to create their own little world, importing thousands of trees and digging deep down into the desert to obtain the earth that would be pushed around to create the rolling topography.

The 17th hole fits right in, with its waterfall tumbling down into a creek to the left of the green and ultimately to the large pond that fronts the putting surface. The tees are set on a ridge looking down at the hole and giving you a good idea of what to avoid—you don't want to be short or left.

No. 9 The Honors Course, Ooltewah, Tennessee

◯

9th Hole, 369 Yards, Par 4

The Honors Course, which opened in 1983, is traditionalist in the sense that it was avowedly created to honor amateur golf. But with Pete Dye as the designer, it is a modern golf course, complete with in-your-face water hazards. One of those is at the 9th hole, crowding the left edge of the green and also guarding the front of the putting surface.

The fairway is wide up until the 235-yard mark, at which point it is narrowed by a grass bunker that with its tangled growth is far more penal than most sand bunkers. This encourages a layup off the tee, leaving a longer approach. Those bailing out to the right on the second shot are fore-warned that the green slopes significantly toward the water. It is not unknown for chip shots to roll across the green and into the hazard.

No. 10 Chambers Bay,
University Place, Washington

◠

2nd Hole, 404 Yards, Par 4

The site of Chambers Bay, the municipal course near Tacoma that will host the 2015 U.S. Open, was a gravel-mining pit before Robert Trent Jones, Jr., and his associates got hold of it and built the layout that opened in 2007.

Much of that sand was pushed around to create artificial (but natural-looking) mounding at this links-style course.

There was more subtle shaping, too, such as the small hummock in the fairway on the 2nd hole. The slope directs balls hit down the center toward the left side, leaving a tougher approach shot over a bunker. A drive to the right side leaves a more favorable approach. Not far behind the green is the course's only tree, with a view of the bay beyond.

No. 11 Huntsville Golf Club, Shavertown, Pennsylvania

⌒

2nd Hole, 391 Yards, Par 4

The feeling at Rees Jones–designed Huntsville in northeast Pennsylvania is one of bucolic isolation, as there are no homes or developments around the course, just acres and acres of forested hills and some farmhouses and barns. The second tee sits some 100 feet above the fairway and offers a splendid vista of that scene.

With the drop in elevation offering the prospect of a long drive, it might be tempting to hit a driver down the left side and leave a short second shot. With large bunkers left of the fairway, that may not be the best idea. A sensible layup that gives a wide berth to those bunkers will still leave a manageable second shot to a well-bunkered green.

No. 12 Club de Golf Valderrama, Sotogrande, Spain

4th Hole, 558 Yards, Par 5

The 17th hole is the most famous par 5 at Valderrama because it comes near the end of the round and is notorious for balls spinning off the green into the water. But the 4th is a much better hole at this Robert Trent Jones–designed course that has hosted a number of professional events, including the 1997 Ryder Cup. Indeed, it is one of the best par 5s in Europe.

The pro or top amateur can get home in two, but only with a pair of shots that combine power with accuracy. To the right of the green is a water hazard complete with a small waterfall. The green is narrow and also elevated, adding to the challenge. To get a reasonable angle to the green, the tee shot needs to be on the left side of the fairway, but there is a large fairway bunker on that side, so it requires a bold drive as well as a bold second shot to conquer this hole. Meanwhile, average golfers will be happy to come away with a par.

No. 13 Terravista Golf Course, Trancoso, Brazil

○

14th Hole, 216 Yards, Par 3

There is still plenty of spectacular land in the world waiting for golf courses to be built, though much of it is in areas where the game does not yet have a strong foothold. One such place is the coast of the Brazilian state of Bahia, where in 2004 American architect Dan Blankenship received the plum assignment of building a course on a piece of property that included 130-foot cliffs facing the Atlantic Ocean.

The postcard hole is the par-3 14th, with a carry across a chasm to a green perched on top of a cliff on the other side. The championship tees are for experts only, but the other tee markers offer a slightly more generous angle without taking the chasm out of play. The three-tiered green is large, especially in width, but that can make two-putting a challenge.

**No. 14 TPC Sawgrass (Stadium Course),
Ponte Vedra Beach, Florida**

↻

14th Hole, 481 Yards, Par 4

TPC Sawgrass is not a long course, but designer Pete Dye believes that pros should at least occasionally need to hit a long (or at least longish) iron into a par 4. Consequently, he stretched this hole to 481 yards in a 2006 renovation of the course that annually hosts the Players Championship.

But there is more to this hole than length. While the fairway is reasonably wide, it's an intimidating tee shot with water down the left side and tall spectator mounds to the right. A long waste bunker traces the water hazard on the left, serving to save some balls from going into the water. The water ends some eighty yards short of the green, but the waste bunker continues all the way to guard the left side of the putting surface. The entrance to the green narrows through a chute of trees, and there are four pot bunkers to the right of the green.

No. 15 Black Diamond Ranch (Quarry Course), Lecanto, Florida

⌒

15th Hole, 358 Yards, Par 4

No. 16 Mission Hills Golf Club (Olazabel Course), Shenzhen, China

⌒

15th Hole, 580 Yards, Par 5

The Quarry Course is so named for a good reason. Part of the layout sits in an old dolomite mine, framed by rock cliffs that give the holes a striking appearance. The 15th hole is the highlight of the Tom Fazio design that opened in 1987, the tee sitting atop one cliff, playing down to a fairway at the bottom, with a green backed by more cliffs.

There is a lake to the left, with a skinny bunker running along the water for the length of the hole. The green is tucked around a corner of the lake, making for a more challenging approach shot, though a manageable one since it is played with a short iron.

See page 220 for photo.

Since it's inception in 1994, Mission Hills has grown from a single course to an even dozen. The Olazabal Course, which opened in 2002, has established itself as a standout in that crowd, as evidenced by its selection to host the World Cup when Mission Hills became the permanent host of the event starting in 2007.

Spanish pro José Maria Olazabal designed the course in collaboration with American architects Lee Schmidt and Brian Curley, who worked on ten of the Mission Hills layouts with various collaborators. The hole is dominated visually by large bunkers in the landing areas for each shot. A long and straight drive gives the player the option of going for the green in two, if he is not intimidated by the expanse of water to the front and left of the putting surface. Those laying up should be sure to avoid the bunkers on the left. It's a frightening shot over water to reach the green from there.

No. 17 Cabo del Sol
(Ocean Course),
Cabo San Lucas, Mexico

17th Hole, 178 Yards, Par 3

Designer Jack Nicklaus calls the stretch of coast where he laid out the final three holes at Cabo del Sol's Ocean Course "the best piece of golf property in the world." He may just be right, and it can't be denied that he rose to the occasion.

The scenically dazzling 17th hole plays across a sandy cove, a bit of the sea, and, lastly, the rock face of the out-cropping on top of which the green sits. There is some leeway between the beach and the green both short and right, so bailing out to the left is not necessary. The hole plays only 137 yards from the regular tees, with a more favorable angle, diminishing the chances that beauty will turn into utter disaster. But two deep bunkers on the right don't make for a completely carefree day at the beach.

No. 18 Kiawah Island Resort
(Ocean Course),
Kiawah Island, South Carolina

18th Hole, 439 Yards, Par 4

This is not the same hole where Bernhard Langer missed a par putt to lose the 1991 Ryder Cup for Europe a year after the course opened. It's better. In 2002, Kiawah Island gained permission to move the green some twenty-five yards to the right, to the dune line, which is where architect Pete Dye had wanted it in the first place.

The hole now plays as a dogleg to the right. If a player wants to flirt with a fairway bunker on the right side, there is the opportunity to catch a downslope and gain distance on the tee shot. The green is now in a more natural setting, slightly elevated, with a great view of the Atlantic.

CLASSIC
HOLES

The golden age of architecture lasted from the end of World War I through the 1920s when the game was expanding in the United States (and also, to a certain extent, in other locales, such as Australia and Europe) and some of the greatest architects in history were plying their trade. Donald Ross, A. W. Tillinghast, and Alister MacKenzie led the way, designing courses that have stood the test of time.

Layouts from that era still dominate lists of greatest courses. But there was plenty of depth, too, in terms of both courses and architects. Designers such as Perry Maxwell, Willie Park, Jr., George Thomas, James Braid, Stanley Thompson, and Harry Colt (the latter represented on other Dream 18s) produced outstanding work. The attribute that all of the designers and most of the courses of the era had in common was making the best use of the natural features of the given property.

While the pace of construction slowed down in the 1930s, a number of great courses continued to be built in a similar style, and are represented here.

This Dream 18 starts strong with three holes by Ross. He and Tillinghast both have four holes in all. MacKenzie, who was not quite as prolific, has two, as does Park, while Maxwell has one of his own and also helped out on two others.

Left: **No. 1 Aronimink Golf Club, Newtown Square, Pennsylvania** ↻ 1st Hole, 430 Yards, Par 4 *See page 238 for description.*

	Par	Black	Blue	White	Gold	Red
1 Aronimink 1	4/5	430	420	412	412	397*
2 Pinehurst (No. 2) 2	4	472	437	410	386	334
3 Wannamoisett 3	3	138	138	127	127	105
4 Crystal Downs 7	4	335	335	330	330	292
5 Colonial 5	4	472	432	432	380	354
6 Baltimore (Five Farms East) 6	5	583	574	566	501	501
7 San Francisco 7	3	189	169	169	169	152
8 Prairie Dunes 8	4	430	417	417	359	359
9 Maidstone 9	4	402	402	370	370	331
Out	35/36	3451	3324	3233	3034	2825

	Par	Black	Blue	White	Gold	Red
10 Winged Foot (West) 10	3	190	183	183	179	179
11 Bel-Air 11	4	392	392	384	366	366
12 Quaker Ridge 6	4/5	446	446	434	424	414*
13 Salem 13	4	342	326	297	268	268
14 Olympia Fields (North) 14	4	444	438	420	410	322
15 Highlands Links 15	5	540	540	530	530	451
16 Gleneagles (King's) 5	3	178	161	149	130	114
17 Royal Melbourne (West) 17	4/5	439	439	428	428	417*
18 Shinnecock Hills 14	4	447	436	436	361	361
In	35/37	3418	3361	3261	3096	2892
TOTAL	**70/73**	**6869**	**6684**	**6494**	**6130**	**5717**

*Par five for women

No. 1 Aronimink Golf Club,
Newtown Square, Pennsylvania

○

1st Hole, 430 Yards, Par 4

The 1st hole at this Donald Ross gem near Philadelphia, which opened in 1928, is considered to be one of the best openers in the game. With the exception of a bunker eighty yards short of the green, there are no fairway bunkers, which might ease the nerves somewhat on the tee shot. Still, this is a tough hole with an uphill second shot. A drive in the right half of the fairway gives a better angle for the approach to a diagonal green on a hole that makes a slight dogleg to the left.

The putting surface is two-tiered, and maintained at a healthy speed. If the hole is located on the front, putts from the back tier have been known to roll right off the green.

See page 236 for photo.

No. 2 Pinehurst Resort and Country Club (No. 2 Course),
Pinehurst, North Carolina

○

2nd Hole, 472 Yards, Par 4

The greens at Pinehurst No. 2 are very difficult to hit because most of them are crowned in the middle and drop off on all sides. At the 2005 U.S. Open, the 2nd hole earned the distinction of being the toughest of them all to hit, with only 30.5 percent finishing on the green in regulation, though many approach shots spent a couple of seconds on the green before rolling off. It's not even an easy green to chip to. Retief Goosen needed two chips on this hole in the final round in 2005, which was the beginning of the end for him as he blew the lead by shooting an 81. Such experiences are by no means uncommon (in fact, Goosen's second chip barely avoided rolling off the surface again).

Ideally, tee shots should favor the left side to leave a better angle for the approach shot. But there are four fairway bunkers on the left, and those are not a good place to be on such a long par 4. The right side of the fairway is devoid of bunkers, but there is one guarding the green from that angle.

Pinehurst No. 2 is the masterpiece of one of America's greatest architects, Donald Ross, who had a home off the third fairway. He first designed the course in 1901, but continued refining it through the years, especially in a 1935 redesign when the course was converted from sand greens to grass. It wasn't until then that greens like the 2nd truly began to take shape.

**No. 3 Wannamoisett Country Club,
Rumford, Rhode Island**

ɔ

3rd Hole, 138 Yards, Par 3

The Donald Ross Society used this hole as the basis for its logo, and what other endorsement is needed? Ross fit Wannamoisett onto just 104 acres, and it plays to a par of 69. The 3rd hole doesn't take up much space. It's a very short iron from the tee, which left Ross free to make the green and its surroundings very challenging though not unfair.

There's a deep bunker covering the entire front of the elevated green and another bunker to the left. There's no bunker to the right, but the drop-off is so steep that none is necessary to make for a challenging recovery shot. And the green is small enough so that it takes a good shot, even with a short iron, to find the target.

No. 4 Crystal Downs Country Club, Frankfort, Michigan

◯

7th Hole, 335 Yards, Par 4

This Alister MacKenzie/Perry Maxwell design opened in 1933 and has emerged from hidden-gem status to be ranked in the top fifteen in the United States in all of the major golf magazine rankings. That's the result of golf architecture devotees making the pilgrimage to northern Michigan and being knocked out by the design.

The 7th hole features a boomerang-shaped green that bends around a right bunker, with a slope in the middle of the green providing a "bank" for balls being putted from one sector to another where there is not a direct line to the hole. Such a green works because it's a short approach shot. The fairway stops at about 215 yards from the tee, so it's a layup and a wedge for most players. You can hit a driver to the bottom of a gully, but then it's a blind approach from the rough and you've also brought a water hazard to the left and a bunker to the right into play. There could be a drive-the-green option, but it is pretty much untested (though interesting to contemplate) since Crystal Downs doesn't host any pro tournaments.

No. 5 Colonial Country Club, Fort Worth, Texas

5th Hole, 472 Yards, Par 4

This is the last of three holes at Colonial known as the "Horrible Horseshoe." Not that they are bad holes, it's just that they might leave some horrible numbers on the scorecard. They are all long holes, and for that you can blame club founder Marvin Leonard, who bought some extra property and had architect Perry Maxwell redesign the 3rd, 4th, and 5th holes the year before Colonial hosted the 1941 U.S. Open. The course had been designed by Texas architect John Bredemus in 1936.

The 5th is not only long, it's tight. Trees and the Trinity River wait to the right of the fairway; a ditch and more trees guard the left. What's more, it bends to the right around the trees at a point that forces long hitters either to lay back with a 3-wood or risk a power fade with the driver. That leaves a long second shot to a green well guarded by three bunkers. It's a hole where the pros are happy to survive with a par.

No. 6 Baltimore Country Club (Five Farms East Course), Timonium, Maryland
◯
6th Hole, 583 Yards, Par 5

It is appropriate that a course at a site called Five Farms should have a hole called the Barn hole. Baltimore Country Club expanded in 1922 from the city to a second location, Five Farms, and hired A. W. Tillinghast to design the course (now known as Five Farms East after a second course was added).

The barn is very much a part of this hole. It's in bounds and stands very close to the fairway just inside the ninety-degree dogleg. It's a 240-yard carry, so long hitters can fly over it and shorten the hole, bringing the green within reach in two shots. It's a three-shot hole when played conventionally—and a long third shot if you can't carry a trio of cross bunkers 170 yards from the green. You don't want to hook your tee shot here, no matter which line you take. If you're cutting the corner, going left means out of bounds. If you're playing it straight, a hook will put you somewhere in the vicinity of the barn.

No. 7 San Francisco Golf Club, San Francisco, California
◯
7th Hole, 189 Yards, Par 3

This is known as the Duel hole because it was built on the site of the last legal duel in the United States, which took place in 1859. That's an interesting fact, but it doesn't have anything to do with why the hole was chosen for this book. It's here because it's one of the best par 3s ever designed by A. W. Tillinghast, one of the game's greatest architects.

It's a downhill hole played to a green guarded by two bunkers on the left, one behind, and one to the right. The green is narrower in the front than in the back, but a ridge bisects the back part of the green and it's a tough putt if you are not on the proper side. However, it's a dangerous shot to the back right portion because you are not shooting at the length of the green.

No. 8 Prairie Dunes Country Club, Hutchinson, Kansas

◠

8th Hole, 430 Yards, Par 4

Located in America's heartland, Prairie Dunes nonetheless has the feel of a Scottish links course with a terrain marked by dunes and weather marked by wind. The 8th hole plays up a series of dunes, the last of them 140 yards from the green. With the prevailing wind into the player and from the left, this hole plays longer than its yardage. That wind also sends weak slices into the tall fescue rough bordering the right side of the fairway.

Most players cannot drive it far enough to have a full view of the flagstick for the second shot. Bunkers to the front right are to be avoided because they are dotted with thick clumps of grass. Reaching the green is not a source of relief, as the two-tiered green is severely rolling—a trademark of designer Perry Maxwell—and easy to three-putt.

**No. 9 Maidstone Club,
East Hampton, New York**

◯

9th Hole, 402 Yards, Par 4

Standing on the 9th tee at Maidstone, the golfer can gaze out at the Atlantic Ocean to his right. When attention is turned to the task at hand, however, the view is much more unsettling. The hole runs between dunes on both the right and left side. The dunes to the left are covered with such thick grass that a lost ball is the probable result of a shot hit there. The dunes to the right aren't much more forgiving.

If you hit a bad drive, a large cross bunker about eighty yards short of the green is in play and you might need to lay up. Greenside, the main concern is a natural-looking but deep bunker known as the Yale Bowl, to the right and also guarding the front right. This is part of a stretch of holes at Maidstone that are as close as it gets to links golf in the United States, so it is appropriate that the course was designed (in 1922) by a Scotsman, Willie Park, Jr.

**No. 10 Winged Foot Golf Club (West Course),
Mamaroneck, New York**

◠

10th Hole, 190 Yards, Par 3

**No. 11 Bel-Air Country Club,
Los Angeles, California**

◠

11th Hole, 392 Yards, Par 4

Ben Hogan once described this A. W. Tillinghast hole as "a 3-iron into some guy's bedroom." The house behind the green that prompted that statement is still there, but it's no longer a 3-iron for the pros. A 7-iron is more like it, which just goes to show what a different game it is these days. While the hole is no longer among the hardest at Winged Foot, it still may be the best.

In fact, the smallish green might be more appropriate as a target for a mid-iron than a long iron. The front, especially, is very narrow, with bunkers guarding both sides. The bunker on the right is very deep. The back of the green is wider, but that's not much comfort when the hole is tucked close to one of the bunkers. And going long is a concern because of the out of bounds (the backyard of that house) behind the green. On top of all of that, the treacherous green is one of the best that Tillinghast ever devised. From many spots on the green, two-putting will take all of a player's skill.

Bel-Air is one of many excellent courses that George Thomas designed in the Los Angeles area, this one with help from William P. Bell and Jack Neville. The 11th hole is on a tract of land across a canyon that came to be used only after part of the original property was lost to the UCLA campus during the design phase in 1925.

The club was developed along with the surrounding area by millionaire Alphonzo E. Bell (no relation to the course co-designer) and the 11th hole is overlooked by mansions of the Bel-Air neighborhood. It is a dogleg to the left that has lost its original alternate fairway but retains its Thomas–designed green, which is long and narrow. The back portion is set at a different angle and is very narrow; when the hole is located there, it takes a very bold shot to fire at the flag.

No. 12 Quaker Ridge Golf Club, Scarsdale, New York

6th Hole, 446 Yards, Par 4

Quaker Ridge is located just up the road from Winged Foot in Westchester County. Not as well known because it has not hosted U.S. Opens, Quaker Ridge had the same designer, A. W. Tillinghast, and many consider it to be architecturally the equal of its neighbor. It's just about as tough, too, especially the 6th hole.

Tillinghast actually redesigned seven holes (including the 6th) of an original nine-hole course by John Duncan Dunn and built eleven of his own. The 6th hole asks a lot of the player. By all but the standards of today's Tour player, it's a long par 4. But it's also narrow, with a fairway only twenty-two yards wide and a creek to the left. The fairway slopes right to left, making it even harder to hit. It also gives the player a lie that promotes a right-to-left draw on an approach that favors a left-to-right fade. Other than that, there's not much to worry about.

No. 13 Salem Country Club, Peabody, Massachusetts

◯

13th Hole, 342 Yards, Par 4

Donald Ross called the 13th green at Salem "the best green I ever designed," and that's saying something. Ben Crenshaw, one of the greatest putters of all time, called it one of his favorite greens in the world. The putting surface is fairly small, but it has three tiers. Find the wrong tier on your approach shot, and two-putting will be a challenge. There are also three bunkers around the green, which drops off on all sides.

The sensible shot off the tee is one of 200 to 230 yards into a bowl of a fairway, leaving an uphill shot to a short hole that is anything but easy.

No. 14 Olympia Fields Country Club
(North Course), Olympia Fields, Illinois

◯

14th Hole, 444 Yards, Par 4

Butterfield Creek cuts across the fairway at the 125-yard mark from the tee and then cuts back across again about 300 yards out. But it's more dangerous where you can't see it: Mostly hidden by trees, the hazard runs up the right side of the fairway to catch pushed or sliced tee shots.

The second shot is uphill to a green flanked by deep bunkers and difficult to putt because of a severe back-to-front slope. Though it is not particularly long, the hole ranked as the third toughest on the Willie Park, Jr.,–designed course at the 2003 U.S. Open, where it played as the 5th hole. It's even harder for the average golfer, who doesn't get much of a break at 420 yards from the regular tees, leaving an uphill fairway wood shot to the green for many players.

No. 15 Highlands Links, Ingonish Beach, Nova Scotia, Canada

◯

15th Hole, 540 Yards, Par 5

Highlands Links was built in 1939 for National Parks of Canada in order to stimulate tourism on Cape Breton Island. Canadian architect Stanley Thompson's course indeed proved to be a draw, and many rate it as the best course in the country.

The 15th features a view of Whale Island in the distance and a design that tempts the better player into a risky route in order to have a chance to get home in two. A drive down the left side of the fairway cuts off a bit of distance but, more important, enables the tee shot to reach a downslope that will propel the ball forward and leave as little as 220 yards to the green. Too far left, though, and the ball will end up in the trees. For those not able to get home in two, there is a series of four fairway bunkers on the left side to catch an errant second shot.

No. 16 The Gleneagles Hotel
(King's Course),
Auchterarder, Scotland

○

5th Hole, 178 Yards, Par 3

The 5th hole at the King's Course at Gleneagles is called Het Girdle, which means "hot griddle." The implication is that just as oil may slide off a hot griddle, an imprecise shot can slide off this green. A long way off the green, as it happens, because the ground plunges steeply down on all sides of the putting surface. There's no such thing as chipping to this green—the only way back up to it is a high pitch shot or a blast from one of the bunkers.

While Scotland is known for its egalitarian links courses, Gleneagles is a departure as it is a five-star inland resort. James Braid, who went on to become a fine golf designer after winning five British Opens, fashioned the King's and Queen's courses in 1919 (the resort also has a more recent Jack Nicklaus–designed course).

**No. 17 Royal Melbourne Golf Club (West Course),
Black Rock, Victoria, Australia**

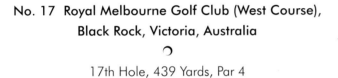

17th Hole, 439 Yards, Par 4

When the members of Royal Melbourne decided to build a new course in 1926, they wanted the best golf architect they could find, so they sent all the way to England for Alister MacKenzie. It was a good decision. MacKenzie made the long trip and gave them a course that is generally considered to be in the top twenty in the world.

Royal Melbourne has some large-scale bunkers, and two of the more impressive ones are to the right of the 17th green, the first one wrapping just a bit around the front. There is also a large fairway bunker to the left of the landing area on the tee shot. These bunkers might be minor nuisances to pros or scratch players, but they can wreak havoc on the average player. Still, MacKenzie thoughtfully kept the left side of the green free of bunkers, so you can steer to that side and be content with bogey or a chance to chip-and-putt for a par.

**No. 18 Shinnecock Hills Golf Club,
Southampton, New York**

14th Hole, 447 Yards, Par 4

Shinnecock Hills needed to redesign its course when a road was routed through a portion of it in the 1920s. It's a good thing for the world of golf that it did, because when William Flynn was commissioned to build a virtually new course, much of it utilizing newly acquired property, he came up with a masterpiece.

When he looked at that new property, Flynn must have been delighted to see the area that is now the 14th hole. He placed the tee up on a ridge, playing down to a bumpy fairway that runs through its own little valley. It's a completely natural hole, enhanced by fairway bunkers on each side. For the second shot, the fairway turns slightly to the right and back uphill to a green that sits on a plateau. You can bounce the ball onto the putting surface, but the shot needs to be accurate, since bunkers at the front pinch in slightly from both sides.

CONTINENTAL EUROPE

HOLES

Courses in Continental Europe tend to get overlooked, since the focus tends to be on Great Britain and Ireland. That's a shame, because the Continent has some excellent seaside golf and some outstanding parkland layouts as well. Top international architects have plied their trade there, particularly Harry Colt before World War II and Robert Trent Jones after.

Spain and Sweden have led the way in producing top European players, and the same is true to a certain extent in courses, particularly Spain. Portugal has become an outstanding golf destination with many fine resort courses, while The

Netherlands has a string of links-style courses on its northern coast. France is perhaps the most underrated nation of all in terms of places to play, and Germany is not to be ignored.

Some European courses are in other lists, so this Dream 18 is not the definitive selection of the best eighteen holes on the Continent. But it's a fine collection of holes from France (four), Portugal (three), Spain (three), Germany (two), Sweden (two), The Netherlands (two), Austria (one), and Italy (one). You'll speak a lot of languages on this course, but perhaps it's fair to say that golf is a universal language in Europe.

Left: **No. 13 Golf de Sperone, Bonifacio, Corsica, France** ☽ 13th Hole, 305 Yards, Par 4 *See page 265 for description.*

	Par	Black	Blue	White	Gold	Red			Par	Black	Blue	White	Gold	Red
1 Kennemer (B) 1	4	450	419	419	362	362	10 Noordwijkse 8		4	406	406	358	306	306
2 Sotogrande 7	4	420	420	363	331	318	11 Les Bordes 11		4	402	380	380	348	293
3 Penha Longa	5	501	486	464	464	441	12 Hamburger 17		5	481	481	474	421	421
(Atlantic) 6							13 Sperone 13		4	305	305	289	262	244
4 Praia D'El Rey 4	4	334	315	301	271	249	14 Le Golf National 15		4	402	402	380	352	336
5 Gut Lärchenhof 4	3	191	174	158	150	134	(Albatross)							
6 San Lorenzo 6	4	425	425	402	328	328	15 Valderrama 15		3	237	201	201	172	161
7 Falsterbo 7	4	319	319	292	292	292	16 Pevero 15		5	525	525	514	500	482
8 La Boulie	3	213	189	189	172	172	17 El Saler 17		3	215	187	187	146	146
(La Vallée) 10							18 Barsebäck		4	435	435	391	369	337
9 Fontana 18	5	545	528	510	493	461	(Masters) 17							
Out	36	3398	3275	3098	2863	2757	**In**		36	3408	3322	3174	2876	2726
							TOTAL		72	6806	6597	6272	5739	5483

No. 1 Kennemer Golf & Country Club (B Course), Zandvoort, The Netherlands

↻

1st Hole, 450 Yards, Par 4

Kennemer's Harry Colt–designed course was extensively damaged by Nazi military operations in World War II, but fortunately the club was able to restore the layout to something very close to the original. It also added a third nine designed by Frank Pennink in 1985.

When playing Colt's 18 (the B and C Courses), this plays as the 1st hole, but it is the 10th hole in the European Tour's KLM Open, which Kennemer has hosted since 2006. There are dunes on either side that tend to collect the ball back toward the fairway, a nice feature on an opening hole. The green is open in front, with one bunker on each side. The only red-light warning on the hole is to avoid the gorse bushes on the right side of the green, a real danger for average players who might be hitting a long iron or fairway wood for their second shot.

No. 2 Real Club de Golf Sotogrande, Sotogrande, Spain

⌒

7th Hole, 420 Yards, Par 4

Sotogrande was the first course Robert Trent Jones designed in Europe, opening in 1964. He later returned to build a second Sotogrande course that eventually split off and became known as Valderrama. While Valderrama gets more attention, Sotogrande is a fine course in its own right, and the 7th is its best hole.

The right-to-left dogleg favors a draw off the tee; in fact, longer hitters might go through the fairway into one of two bunkers if they hit it straight. Trees line the left side. The approach shot is even more challenging, with a narrow green surrounded by four bunkers and a pond to the right. Anything to the right kicks down into the water, unless you are lucky enough to catch one of two bunkers on that side.

No. 3 Penha Longa Hotel & Golf Resort (Atlantic Course), Linho, Portugal

⌒

6th Hole, 501 Yards, Par 5

Players who are long enough and bold enough to go for the green in two need to avoid the pond that sits to the left of the green here and must be carried on a shot played from the landing area for tee shots. That's sound golf design from Robert Trent Jones, Jr., but not particularly unusual. What's different here is the obstacle to the right of the green, where a fourteenth-century stone aqueduct stands close enough to the putting surface to be a factor.

A more conventional way to play the hole is as a bit of a double dogleg, hitting your second shot to the right of the pond and approaching the green from there. Since the aqueduct follows the angle of the fairway from that direction, it shouldn't get in the way. Then again, golfers aren't always accurate, so you never know.

No. 4 Praia D'El Rey Golf & Beach Resort, Obidos, Portugal

4th Hole, 334 Yards, Par 4

Praia D'El Rey enjoys an excellent seaside setting and cleverly designed holes like the 4th, a short par 4 with well-placed bunkers. There is a long one cut into a dune on the left starting at 275 yards from the championship tee and extending all the way to the green. On the right side, a bunker cuts into the fairway from the 230- to 260-yard mark. These bunkers create all sorts of options: You can lay up short of the first bunker to the widest part of the fairway, steer left of it but stay short of the second, or (if you have the distance) try to carry the one on the right and not hit a hook that catches the one on the left.

The course was designed by Cabell Robinson, a Spain-based American architect, and opened in 1997.

No. 5 Golf Club Gut Lärchenhof, Cologne, Germany

⌒

4th Hole, 191 Yards, Par 3

Gut Lärchenhof, which dates from 1997, is the only Jack Nicklaus–designed course in Germany and serves as the host of the Mercedes-Benz Championship on the European Tour. Perhaps it is no surprise that Nicklaus would build a hole with similarities to the 16th at Augusta National, considering the success that he has had there. There is a pond to the left of a green that wraps slightly around the back of the hazard. The water is a major factor when the hole is located on the back left of the green. But it is also in the player's mind when the pin is in the front, because that part of the green is narrower, so the tendency is to bail out to the right.

**No. 6 San Lorenzo Golf Club,
Almancil, Portugal**

⌒

6th Hole, 425 Yards, Par 4

The Algarve is Portugal's prime golf region, and San Lorenzo is its most acclaimed course. Designed by America's Joe Lee and opened in 1988, the layout starts out in the trees but comes out into the open on the 6th hole when it reaches the lake formed by the Ria Formosa, making the wind a definite factor.

The hole starts out toward the water and then turns to the left to run alongside the hazard the rest of the way to the green. There are some trees at the corner to prevent cutting the dogleg, but a draw off the tee will work nicely here. You don't want to go to the right on either shot, but a greenside bunker might actually save you from a visit to the water on the approach.

No. 7 Falsterbo Golf Club, Falsterbo, Sweden

☽

7th Hole, 319 Yards, Par 4

Situated on the southern tip of Sweden, Falsterbo plays over a mix of marshland and dune land. The latter is reminiscent of a Scottish links, and that's where the 7th hole lies. This is one of two holes remaining from an original nine-hole course designed by Robert Turnball in 1909, which was mostly lost in a 1930 expansion to eighteen holes.

It's a short par 4 with a dogleg to the left, but any thoughts a long hitter might have of cutting the corner and shooting for the vicinity of the green are tempered by out of bounds to the left and the fact that the green is fronted by (and surrounded by) bunkers. It still represents a birdie chance played conventionally, but those six bunkers around a fairly small green must be avoided.

No. 8 Golf de la Boulie (La Vallée Course), Versailles, France

○

10th Hole, 213 Yards, Par 3

La Boulie's La Vallée Course is among the early courses established in Continental Europe, dating back to 1901 and designed by Scots Willie Park, Jr., and Seymour Dunn. It hosted the French Open as early as 1906 and as late as 1986, with some of the winners there including Walter Hagen, Byron Nelson, Nick Faldo, and Seve Ballesteros. The Racing Club de France now owns the forty-five-hole complex.

The 10th hole is an attractive, downhill par 3 with tall trees behind the green serving as a backdrop. Tightly guarded on three sides by large bunkers, with so little space between them, anything short, left, or right is almost guaranteed to be in the sand, unless it is wide of the bunkers.

No. 9 Golf und Sport Club Fontana, Oberwaltersdorf, Austria

◯

18th Hole, 545 Yards, Par 5

Standing on the 18th tee at Fontana, you can see the green sitting some 390 yards away across a large lake. Of course, not even Bubba Watson can carry the ball that far, so even the longest hitters have to follow the fairway in a left-to-right boomerang shape around the water. It's a fine risk/reward hole for the pros at the European Tour's Bank Austria Open.

An aggressive line cutting off more water from the tee makes the green accessible in two shots, but the water lurks in front, to the right, and behind the green to gobble up any mistakes.

Most amateurs will play this hole more safely to get home in three. But there is a group of bunkers to the left of the fairway on the tee shot and then a large bunker jutting in to cut off the fairway before a second landing area, so even the conservative route isn't stress-free on this hole designed by Canada's Doug Carrick and Austria's Hans Erhard.

No. 10 Noordwijkse Golf Club, Noordwijk, The Netherlands

8th Hole, 406 Yards, Par 4

Noordwijkse plays through both forest and linksland near the North Sea, with the 8th hole returning to the links terrain after a visit to the trees. The hole plays up a rise, and then the fairway bends to the left after proceeding between a pair of dunes. Long hitters may be able to cut the corner over the dune on the left. A pot bunker guards the right front of the green.

The club dates to 1915, but the current course dates to 1972, when it moved to a new site and expanded to eighteen holes. England's Frank Pennink did the design, and the course has hosted a number of Dutch Opens over the years.

No. 11 Les Bordes, Saint-Laurent-Nouan, France

○

11th Hole, 402 Yards, Par 4

Les Bordes was built in 1986 on the estate of Baron Marcel Bich, of Bic pen fame. Designed by American Robert von Hagge, it quickly joined the ranks of Europe's very best courses in terms of design, conditioning, and difficulty. It was purchased by an international group in 2008, with plans for von Hagge to upgrade the course.

Much of the Les Bordes property was originally marshland. With those areas converted to ponds and lakes, the course is both a beauty and very dangerous, with water in play on twelve holes. That includes the 11th, a strategic dogleg to the left. Players can try to shorten the hole by flying over a fairway bunker, but that brings a finger of the lake on the left into play. The advantage is that it shortens an approach shot that must be played over another finger of the same lake directly in front of the green.

No. 12 Hamburger Golf Club, Hamburg, Germany

⌒

17th Hole, 481 Yards, Par 5

No. 13 Golf de Sperone, Bonifacio, Corsica, France

⌒

13th Hole, 305 Yards, Par 4

What gorse is to Scottish courses, a native version called *heide* is to Hamburger, and it is integral to the design of the 17th hole. A field of *heide* interrupts the fairway for about 90 yards, ending at about 405 yards from the championship tee. Regular golfers might face a decision on whether to attempt the carry on the second shot (the middle tees make the hole play only seven yards shorter) or lay up and hit a third shot of some 170 yards.

The better player won't have to worry about the heide after a good tee shot, but he might if he finds a bunker or trees with his drive. This hole, dating from 1930 and designed by England's Harry Colt, is on the verge of being a par 4 for the ace player, owing to the distance gains in the game. The catch is that the fairway makes a fairly early turn to the left by today's standards, which means that the longer hitter needs to hit a draw to stay in the fairway or hit less than a driver off the tee. If he hits the draw and over-does it, a fairway bunker will catch him on the left side.

The hole is just a shade over 300 yards from the championship tee, but not even Tiger Woods would have a go at the green here. An inlet of the Mediterranean juts in front of the green, and even if you can make the 285-yard carry, there's no way to stop the ball on the putting surface. The sea is on the right, too, and there's a downslope to thick bushes behind the green.

Be content to hit a long iron or fairway wood to have the best angle to shoot at the small green on the Robert Trent Jones–designed hole. It should be stress-free that way, and you'll be able to enjoy the lovely view.

See page 252 for photo.

No. 14 Le Golf National (Albatross Course), Guyancourt, France

◯

15th Hole, 402 Yards, Par 4

The Albatross Course at Le Golf National was built in 1990 specifically to host the French Open. The course was designed by Hubert Chesneau of France and Robert von Hagge of the United States, and is known for a demanding finishing stretch of four holes.

That stretch starts with the 15th, a medium-length par 4 where it is imperative not to go to the right on either the first or second shots, as a large pond borders the fairway on that side. The green is on an island, and a hole located on the front portion is extremely dangerous, guarded as it is by water on three sides. If you are going to miss this green, make sure it is to the left and past the front third of the green. Otherwise, you will be taking a penalty stroke.

No. 15 Club de Golf Valderrama, Sotogrande, Spain

◯

15th Hole, 237 Yards, Par 3

This is a long par 3, but the green is fairly narrow, so you need to be accurate with a long iron or fairway wood, or else you will be scrambling for a par here. There are three large bunkers, with the one at the right front the most ominous. The green is open in front, but with another bunker at the left front, the shot has to be accurate to squeeze through the opening. The back right position on the deep green is the most difficult: In order to get close, the tee shot must carry the right bunker, and that part of the green is particularly difficult to putt.

Valderrama, designed by Robert Trent Jones, is rated by many as the top course in Continental Europe and has hosted the European Tour's season-ending Volvo Masters on a number of occasions.

No. 16 Pevero Golf Club, Porto Servo, Italy

⌒

15th Hole, 525 Yards, Par 5

Pevero was designed by Robert Trent Jones and became the first course on the island of Sardinia when it opened in 1972. Part of the posh Costa Smeralda region, Pevero is located on a hill overlooking both the gulf of Pevero and the bay of Cala di Volpe.

The 15th hole provides a lovely view of the bay to the left as it proceeds first downhill, then uphill. Owing to the slope, long hitters will have a harder time reaching it in two than the yardage indicates. In fact, accuracy is most important here as the fairway is lined on both sides by macchia bushes that are so thick as to be practically impenetrable. The green is small, crowned, and ringed by five bunkers.

No. 17 Campo de Golf El Saler, Olivia, Spain

⌒

17th Hole, 215 Yards, Par 3

Javier Arana was Spain's top golf architect, and it is widely acknowledged that El Saler is his best course. Located on the Mediterranean near Valencia, El Saler opened in 1968 and has several holes that are reminiscent of Scottish links.

One of those is the 17th, which plays directly toward the sea. The green is reasonably large, as befits a par 3 of this length, but is surrounded by bunkers and dunes and is not easy to hit on a windswept day.

No. 18 Barsebäck Golf & Country Club
(Masters Course),
Malmö, Sweden

☽

17th Hole, 435 Yards, Par 4

Barsebäck has been the site of the European Tour's Scandinavian Masters and the 2003 Solheim Cup. Those tournaments were held on what was a composite of the resort's two courses, but that 18 has now been pulled together for regular play and is known as the Masters Course. The 17th hole was part of the original course designed by Swede Ture Bruce in 1969, and was redesigned by England's Donald Steel in 1989.

The 17th plays through a forest, so there will be tree trouble for a drive that strays too far right or left. The green is very deep and is guarded by a single bunker, a large one on the left side that eats into the center of the putting surface. The prevailing wind is in the player's face, coming off the Øresund, the body of water separating Sweden and Denmark, which is only a few hundred yards away from the green.

AUSTRALIA/NEW ZEALAND

HOLES

Next to the United States, golf has taken deeper root in Australia and New Zealand than anywhere else in the world since being exported from the British Isles.

Of course, the fact that they were British colonies helped. So did the type of land that exists near Melbourne, which happens to be perfect for golf courses. By the 1920s most of Melbourne's golf clubs had migrated from city sites out to the nearby Sandbelt. While not quite linksland, the sandy soil is perfect for the creation of courses. Perhaps nowhere in the world is there such a collection of outstanding courses in such a small area, with Royal Melbourne as the standout.

Australia was also fortunate in having the great architect Alister MacKenzie visit to design Royal Melbourne in 1926. While in the country, he moonlighted on advising a bevy of other courses that were in their formative stages or had just opened, and he also designed New South Wales near Sydney.

The majority of the courses on this Dream 18 are either in the Melbourne area or extensions of that area to the southeast (the Mornington Peninsula) or southwest (Barwon Heads), the latter areas offering opportunities for true links courses of recent vintage. This list represents the cream of the Australia/New Zealand crop, except for the omission of Barnbougle Dunes and Royal Adelaide, each of which have holes in two other Dream 18s (Barnbougle Dunes in Short Holes and Strategic Holes; Royal Adelaide in Hard Holes and Bunkerless Holes).

Left: **No. 18 Kauri Cliffs, Matauri Bay, New Zealand** ↻ 17th Hole, 475 Yards, Par 4 *See page 287 for description.*

	Par	Black	Blue	White	Gold	Red			Par	Black	Blue	White	Gold	Red
1 Thirteenth Beach 13	4	353	342	342	342	316		10 Commonwealth 17	4	338	338	328	328	315
2 Metropolitan 5	4	420	391	391	344	344		11 Cape Kidnappers 17	4	465	440	422	393	366
3 Peninsula (North) 2	3	177	177	167	167	139		12 Palm Meadows 18	5	575	552	552	494	494
4 Gulf Harbour 16	4	466	433	413	413	315		13 Paraparaumu Beach 17	4	444	444	423	423	329
5 New South Wales 5	5	515	515	490	473	473		14 National (Old) 7	3	153	153	133	118	111
6 Kingston Heath 6	4	442	423	423	384	384		15 National (Moonah) 2	5	547	505	505	479	443
7 Newcastle 7	3	163	163	163	141	141		16 Royal Melbourne (West) 6	4	450	428	428	369	369
8 Ellerston 7	4	451	421	421	390	390		17 The Dunes 17	3	197	197	161	161	117
9 Victoria 9	5	615	562	562	562	547		18 Kauri Cliffs 17	4	475	443	408	408	372
Out	36	3602	3427	3372	3216	3049		**In**	36	3644	3500	3360	3173	2916
								TOTAL	**72**	**7246**	**6927**	**6732**	**6389**	**5965**

No. 1 Thirteenth Beach Golf Links (Beach Course),
Barwon Heads, Victoria, Australia

⌒

13th Hole, 353 Yards, Par 4

The 13th hole at the Thirteenth Beach Golf Links Beach Course runs parallel to the beach of that name, just a couple of hundred yards away. The course, which opened in 2001, is blessed with genuine links terrain, especially this corner of it.

The left side of the 13th fairway is bordered by a sandy wasteland, with scattered tea trees. On the right side, architect Tony Cashmore placed a nest of six small bunkers at about 240 yards from the back tee (230 from the regular tee). With the fairway narrowing at this point, and more bunkers a little farther along, there is little reason to try to overpower this hole. It's just a short iron to a green featuring only one bunker, but it's a small, three-tiered putting surface that is not easy either to hit or to putt on.

No. 2 Metropolitan Golf Club, South Oakleigh, Victoria, Australia

○

5th Hole, 420 Yards, Par 4

A not-so-famous Mackenzie and a world-renowned MacKenzie are responsible for this hole. First came J.B. Mackenzie, an engineer who was a member of Metropolitan when the club moved from its city location out to the suburbs in 1908. He did an excellent job laying out a course in the sand hills, one that was refined in 1926 when famed architect Alister MacKenzie made a visit to Australia and advised the club on bunkering and some minor routing changes.

The 5th hole features a bunker to the right of the fairway that bothers short and medium hitters, and a pair of bunkers to the left that are in play for the better player. Because of a significant right-to-left slope on the green, it's an advantage to play your approach shot from the left side of the fairway. Your work isn't done once you get to the green—Metropolitan is known for maintaining some of the slickest putting surfaces in the world.

No. 3 The Peninsula Country Golf Club (North Course), Frankston, Victoria, Australia

○

2nd Hole, 177 Yards, Par 3

The Peninsula Country Golf Club has thirty-six holes dating to the late 1960s, when it moved to a new site in Frankston, close to the Mornington Peninsula and about forty minutes from Melbourne. Designed by local Sloan Morpeth, the South Course was always considered the stronger of the two, but after Michael Clayton redesigned all thirty-six holes in 2002, the shorter but more interesting North Course became the darling of course critics, moving into the top twenty in the country.

The 2nd hole at the North is modeled on the 5th at Royal Melbourne West, playing over a valley from a tee on one hill to a green on another. The green is well guarded on both sides by standard bunkers and by a scrubby, sandy waste area beyond. And the slope in front of the green means that the tee shot needs to carry all the way to the putting surface.

No. 4 Gulf Harbour Country Club,
Whangaparaoa, New Zealand

◠

16th Hole, 466 Yards, Par 4

There are two routes on this hole. The safe route is to play around the ravine, staying to the left of it on the tee shot and then turning to the right to play down the peninsula to the green. It's a long hole that way, so those with adequate length and courage may opt to hit their tee shots over Okoromai Bay and have a shorter approach shot. Missing to the right is not recommended on either route, but the gambling route is complicated by a group of tall trees that must be avoided. The green, guarded by a bunker on the right, is on a scenic spot at the end of the peninsula.

The Robert Trent Jones, Jr.,–designed course near Auckland has hosted the 1998 World Cup and several New Zealand Opens.

No. 5 New South Wales Golf Club, Le Perouse, New South Wales, Australia

◠

5th Hole, 515 Yards, Par 5

The view on the tee shot on this hole is intimidating; the view after that is inspiring. The tee shot is played over an area of scrub brush and over a valley. The only part of the fairway that can be seen is a sharp rise, the top of which is 250 yards from the championship tee and 225 yards from the regular tee. Once you reach that promised land (with the tee shot, it is hoped), you look down at a fairway

plunging down to a green set on the brink of Botany Bay behind it. It's a drop of ninety feet from the ridge to the putting surface.

Long hitters can catch part of that downslope with their drives, bringing the green into the range of an iron shot. It's a big advantage to be able to fly an iron into the green, because deep bunkers guard the left front. A run-up second shot works only on the right side, but if you go too far to the right, you catch another bunker. For those who can't get home in two or choose to lay up on this Alister MacKenzie hole, the right side of the fairway leaves the best angle for a wedge to the green.

No. 6 Kingston Heath Golf Club, Moorabbin, Victoria, Australia
○
6th Hole, 442 Yards, Par 4

When Alistair MacKenzie visited Australia in 1926, he devised the bunkering for the recently opened Kingston Heath layout designed by Dan Soutar. MacKenzie outdid himself on the 6th hole. This hole is trouble for players who slice the ball or who struggle out of bunkers. For those who fit into both categories, it can be a nightmare, but it's an outstanding hole nonetheless.

The hole is marked by two groups of bunkers to the right—seven in the landing area for tee shots and five next to the green, coming in an array of shapes and sizes. On the left side, there is only one fairway bunker and another bunker a little bit short of the green, though both are large. There are also bushes to the left of the fairway landing area and a grass depression to the left of the green, so the 6th is a tough hole all-around.

No. 7 Newcastle Golf Club, Fern Bay, New South Wales, Australia
○
7th Hole, 163 Yards, Par 3

Distance control is a must on the 7th hole at Newcastle. Two very deep bunkers in front of the green are the first thing you notice from the tee. That tends to put the "don't be short" thought in your head, but in fact, going over the green is as bad or worse. Behind the green is a steep, closely mown bank that will carry your ball away from the putting surface and leave you with a pitch shot to a green that slopes sharply away from you.

Newcastle, with a course designed by Australia's Eric Apperly in 1937, is off the beaten path, about two hours north of Sydney, but it enjoys an excellent location between the Hunter River and the Pacific Ocean.

**No. 8 Ellerston Golf Course,
Ellerston, Australia**

○

7th Hole, 451 Yards, Par 4

The tee shot is an intimidating one that must be played directly down Pages Creek for much of its length until reaching the safety of the fairway. It's a longer carry the farther to the right you go, so the player who pushes, slices,

or just gets too ambitious will be teeing up another ball and playing his third shot. But if you go too far left, there is a large fairway bunker on that side.

The second shot is more straightforward, though it's not a piece of cake by any means. It is a long iron or fairway wood to a green featuring the creek on the right, a bunker on the right, and two bunkers on the left. The course was designed by Greg Norman and his partner, Bob Harrison, for the use of the Kerry Packer family and their guests.

No. 9 Victoria Golf Club, Cheltenham, Victoria, Australia

9th Hole, 615 Yards, Par 5

The prominent features on the 9th at Victoria are a pair of rises along the way from tee to green. Ideally, the player carries the first rise with his tee shot and the second rise with his second shot, leaving a short iron to the green. Fail to carry the rises, and it will be a long third shot—if you can even get to the green in three. This is one of those Australian courses that has only men's and ladies' tee markers, with the men's tees the equivalent of championship tees on the scorecard. While the tees aren't usually set all the way back, except for tournaments, this is a long hole no matter where you put the markers (it's 547 yards from the ladies' tee).

Victoria was designed by club founder William Meader and club captain Oscar Damman, with an assist on the bunkering from Alister MacKenzie before the course opened in 1927. There are a couple of impressive MacKenzie bunkers at the front right and front left of the green. By the way, accuracy is needed as well as length here, with trees along both sides of the fairway.

**No. 10 Commonwealth Golf Club,
South Oakleigh, Victoria, Australia**

17th Hole, 338 Yards, Par 4

Accuracy is important off the tee on this hole, so the player should think twice about taking a driver and blasting it as close to the green as possible. The key here is to be on the right half of the fairway. That is a much better angle of approach, because you don't have to deal with the greenside bunker on the left.

In fact, the left side is just bad all around. Not only is there the bunker to worry about, the contours of the green make an approach from that side more difficult. There are also trees that jut into the fairway on the left that you might have to hit over, or from among, on the second shot.

No. 11 Cape Kidnappers, Hawke's Bay, New Zealand

17th Hole, 465 Yards, Par 4

Tom Doak is not known for building long courses, but that doesn't mean he doesn't turn the screws on the player with a long hole every once in a while. At the 17th at Cape Kidnappers, a strikingly scenic course on the New Zealand coast, he has produced what could be called a par 4 1/2. Not only is it a long hole, it is uphill. Besides that, there is a nest of six bunkers fronting the green, so you have to be able to fly the ball to the putting surface to get there in regulation.

Here is where the half par comes in. The fairway divides near the green, so if you feel you can't reach the green, you can shoot to the right fairway and try to get a par with a pitch and a putt from there. The left fairway also extends nearly to the green, so after a poor drive you can hit to near the end of that fairway and pitch over the bunkers to the green. The hole may beat you up, but at least you had options.

**No. 12 Palm Meadows Golf Course,
Carrara, Queensland, Australia**

◠

18th Hole, 575 Yards, Par 5

Palm Meadows is a few miles from the ocean on Australia's
Gold Coast, but you'll find plenty of water on the course in
the form of lakes. In fact, water hazards come into play on
fifteen holes on the layout designed by Graham Marsh and
Robin Nelson.

The 18th is most assuredly one of those, but on this

hole the water is as much strategic as it is penal. The
hole bends sharply from left to right around a lake, and
while most mortals are content to play it as a three-shot
hole, it does offer long hitters a chance to get there in
two if they take a bold line over the water on their tee
shot. An inlet of the lake cuts in front of the green, too,
so there is an element of risk on the second shot as well
if a player wants to go for glory. It can be done. In fact,
Australian pro Rodger Davis won a sudden-death playoff
over Curtis Strange here with an eagle at the 1990 Palm
Meadows Cup.

No. 13 Paraparaumu Beach Golf Club,
Paraparaumu Beach,
New Zealand

◯

17th Hole, 444 Yards, Par 4

Paraparaumu Beach sits a few blocks away from the ocean and is surrounded by development, yet the Alex Russell design is as close to authentic linksland as can be found outside the British Isles. It's a course featuring a lot of brown grasses, bumpy fairways, and firm turf that provides a lot of roll.

The 17th hole has a split fairway that provides options, mostly for the short and medium hitter. The right fairway takes a more direct line to the green, but it's a worse angle of approach because a pair of bunkers must be carried or threaded on the second shot. The left route plays longer, but the average player may elect to play it as a three-shot hole that way, with a relatively simple pitch for the third shot. A long hitter can drive it through the right fairway, which is interrupted by a stretch of mounds and rough, so he will generally stay to the left—unless, perhaps, the wind is against.

No. 14 The National Golf Club (Old Course),
Cape Schanck, Victoria, Australia

↻

7th Hole, 153 Yards, Par 3

While Melbourne's top old clubs are concentrated in the Sandbelt about a half hour southeast of the city, the newer National Golf Club extended the range out farther and onto the Mornington Peninsula, about ninety minutes from Melbourne. Launched in 1986, the National has grown to three courses and has taken its place among the outstanding clubs in the country. The original layout, now called the Old Course, was designed by Robert Trent Jones, Jr., and received a lot of attention for its beautiful 7th hole.

The National is located on similar, but more rugged, terrain than the Sandbelt layouts and is closer to the sea. The 7th at the Old Course plays over a lush ravine, with drop-offs also on the left side and behind the green, so the only place to miss the small putting surface by more than a few yards and still find your ball is to the right. It's a short hole, but with the prevailing wind coming off the ocean behind the green, taking an extra club off the tee is often necessary.

No. 15 The National Golf Club (Moonah Course), Cape Schanck, Australia

2nd Hole, 547 Yards, Par 5

Australian golf icon Greg Norman co-designed the National's Moonah Course with partner Bob Harrison in 2000, and perhaps it is a hole where only a player with the power and bravado of the Shark would be tempted to go for the green in two. The hole makes a bend to the right in the final sixty yards, so it's possible for a very long player to cut the corner and get to the green. But the putting surface is at an angle to the player from the tee-shot landing area, making it a fairly shallow target. There's a bigger stop sign in the form of a very deep bunker at the right front.

As the club's course guide states, "More pars and birdies will be made by a tee shot into the fairway, followed by an iron shot second to the heart of the fairway between the final framework of bunkers, located at pitching distance from the green, without succumbing to the temptation of attacking the green directly for two." It goes on to add, "Gorillas excepted!" Sharks, too?

No. 16 Royal Melbourne (West Course),
Black Rock,
Victoria, Australia

⌒

6th Hole, 450 Yards, Par 4

The 6th green is considered the most difficult at Royal Melbourne's West Course, and that is saying something. The putting surfaces designed by Alister MacKenzie are large, very undulating, and kept very fast. Three-putting is common, and four-putting is not as rare as it is on other courses. Because of its slopes, the 6th is also a tough green to chip to. Ernie Els was almost derailed on the way to winning the 2004 Heineken Classic when he took one greenside bunker shot and two chips to reach the green on the way to a triple bogey.

Some of the challenge off the tee has been lessened for top players by the fact that they can pretty easily carry a nest of scraggly bunkers on the inside of the dogleg right, though it's a hole that can play long for the mid-handicapper who has to steer to the left of them. The right side of the fairway is the place to be, because then you don't have to hit over a very deep bunker that fronts the elevated green on the left side.

No. 17 The Dunes Golf Links, Rye, Victoria, Australia
⟳
17th Hole, 197 Yards, Par 3

No. 18 Kauri Cliffs, Matauri Bay, New Zealand
⟳
17th Hole, 475 Yards, Par 4

The Dunes is true to its "links" name, winding through the sand hills of the Mornington Peninsula. Australian architect Tony Cashmore completely reworked an existing layout to create what is now considered to be the best public course in Australia.

The 17th hole has a backdrop of hills covered in brown fescue grasses, with fescue waving in the breeze to the left and right, too. Not that you have to worry about hitting into the stuff on this par 3, it just adds to the links atmosphere. The hole itself is dominated by bunkering. The lip of a bunker sitting in front of the right portion of the green actually rises well above the green's surface. On the lower left side of the plateau green is a group of unkempt-looking bunkers in an area dotted with clumps of native grasses. Tom Watson has called this "an exquisite golf hole," and as the winner of five British Opens, he knows links golf.

The 17th at Kauri Cliffs bends gently right to left around a ravine for its entire length. While it's tempting to challenge the ravine from the tee and get closer to the green on such a long par 4, it's important not to bite off more than you can chew. Playing safely to the right side is not bad: The green is very deep and reasonably wide, so it will accept an approach with a fairway wood or long iron. Even if you can't get there in two, you'll have a fair chance at an up-and-down par.

The high-end resort course developed by Wall Street financier Julian Robertson opened in 2000, with ocean views and a David Harman–designed course to attract visitors to this remote part of northeast New Zealand.

See page 270 for photo.

THE ULTIMATE

DREAM 18

The Ultimate Dream 18 is more than just an all-star listing of holes. It's a mythical course where the hole numbers correspond to the hole numbers in real life, i.e., the first hole is a real first hole, the second hole a real second hole, etc. And it's an 18 that is designed to fit together to create the ultimate round of golf—if you somehow could be transported instantly from each green to the next tee hundreds or thousands of miles away.

This course has been created with a mix of par 3s, 4s, and 5s to make it a par 71 (and a par 73 for women). Within the par 3s, 4s, and 5s, there is a mix of distances to create a variety of shots and challenges. There is variety in the types of strategic options and in the hazards that must be avoided along the way. All corners of the world are represented, as are all eras of architecture.

It's not designed to be the hardest course in the world, though it's plenty tough. It's not designed to be the most scenic, though it may be just that. It is designed to be the ultimate imaginary golf course that "plays" like a real one—a course that, if it existed, would be the best in the world.

Left: **No. 7 Nirwana Bali Golf Club, Tabanan, Bali, Indonesia** ↻ 7th Hole, 214 Yards, Par 3 Scenic Holes *See page 291 for description.*

	Par	Black	Blue	White	Gold	Red			Par	Black	Blue	White	Gold	Red
1 Machrihanish 1	4/5	436	436	428	428	422*		10 Riviera 10	4	315	315	301	275	275
2 Kiawah Island (Ocean) 2	5	543	528	501	495	419		11 Ballybunion (Old) 11	4	451	451	400	384	346
3 Oakmont 3	4	428	390	378	339	339		12 Augusta National 12	3	155	155	145	145	145
4 Spyglass Hill 4	4	370	358	345	345	299		13 Pacific Dunes 13	4	444	390	390	371	336
5 Loch Lomond 5	3	190	175	150	150	110		14 St. Andrews (Old) 14	5	618	530	530	487	487
6 Royal Melbourne (West) 6	4	450	428	428	369	369		15 Somerset Hills 15	4	394	394	375	301	301
7 Nirwana Bali 7	3	214	194	194	144	130		16 Cypress Point 16	3	231	231	219	208	208
8 Prairie Dunes 8	4	430	417	417	359	359		17 National GL 17	4	375	375	350	350	319
9 Royal County Down 9	4/5	486	486	428	428	434*		18 Pebble Beach 18	5	543	543	532	509	455
Out	35/37	3547	3412	3269	3057	2881		**In**	36	3526	3384	3242	3030	2664
								TOTAL	71/73	7073	6796	6511	6087	5545

*Par five for women

No. 1 Machrihanish Golf Club, Campbeltown, Scotland

⌒

1st Hole, 436 Yards, Par 4

Links Holes

The greatest setting for a first tee in the game, it's located on a spit of land jutting out onto a beach. That positioning sets up a drive over the beach, where you can choose how much or how little of the hazard you want to try to carry.

No. 2 Kiawah Island Golf Resort (Ocean Course), Kiawah Island, South Carolina

⌒

2nd Hole, 543 Yards, Par 5

Strategic Holes

There's a lot of strategy on this hole, and not just whether to go for it in two. That's an option for long hitters; others must decide whether to carry a marsh 120 yards short of the green with their second shot.

No. 3 Oakmont Country Club, Oakmont, Pennsylvania

⌒

3rd Hole, 428 Yards, Par 4

Well-Bunkered Holes

A unique and famous hazard lurks on the left side of the fairway, the "Church Pews" bunker. There are also five bunkers on the right side, so you need to be straight here.

No. 4 Spyglass Hill Golf Course, Pebble Beach, California

ↄ

4th Hole, 370 Yards, Par 4

Holes Anyone Can Play

The hole turns to the left through a sandy waste area, setting up a short-iron approach to a green that is fifty yards long but still a shallow target because it is set at an angle to the fairway.

No. 5 Loch Lomond Golf Club, Luss, Scotland

ↄ

5th Hole, 190 Yards, Par 3

Modern Holes

Loch Lomond is a lovely backdrop for this hole that features a long, narrow green with a ridge running through the middle of it.

No. 6 Royal Melbourne (West Course), Black Rock, Victoria, Australia

ↄ

6th Hole, 450 Yards, Par 4

Australia/New Zealand Holes

The green is very difficult because of its many undulations and the speed at which it is maintained. If you miss the elevated putting surface, sometimes just getting your chip or bunker shot to stay on the green is an accomplishment.

No. 7 Nirwana Bali Golf Club, Tabanan, Bali, Indonesia

◯

7th Hole, 214 Yards, Par 3

Scenic Holes

No real worries about the carry over the ocean here, because there is room in front of the green, but going left is a definite no-no, as you will find lush tropical vegetation at the top of a cliff or fall onto the beach below. Farther to the left, on a small island, is a Hindu sea temple where you can pray to the golf gods.

No. 8 Prairie Dunes Country Club, Hutchinson, Kansas

◯

8th Hole, 430 Yards, Par 4

Classic Holes

A slice of Scotland in Middle America, the 8th hole here plays up a series of dunes and leaves most players without a full view of the flagstick for their second shot. Beware of the long fescue grass to the right, and also of the rollicking green.

No. 9 Royal County Down, Newcastle, Northern Ireland

◯

9th Hole, 486 Yards, Par 4

Long Holes

This hole is seriously long, so you might not mind that a downhill slope in the landing area makes the tee shot a blind one. But you won't like it if you drive to the right and your view of the green is blocked by a large dune.

No. 10 Riviera Country Club,
Pacific Palisades, California

◯

10th Hole, 315 Yards, Par 4

Short Holes

It's a tantalizing hole for long hitters because it's downhill and they know they can reach the green in one, even though it's not a high-percentage play to a small, diagonal green. Laying up to the left side of the fairway offers a good birdie chance.

No. 11 Ballybunion Golf Club (Old Course),
Ballybunion, Ireland

◯

11th Hole, 451 Yards, Par 4

Links Holes

On many links courses, the sea is merely a nearby presence that doesn't come into play. That's not the case here, as an inaccurate tee shot can easily find the beach on the right. The beach represents the only sand on the hole, though; there are no bunkers.

No. 12 Augusta National Golf Club, Augusta, Georgia

◯

12th Hole, 155 Yards, Par 3

Strategic Holes

Rae's Creek in front of the green wouldn't be such a factor if it wasn't on a diagonal and the green wasn't so shallow. The combination means that it isn't only a short shot that falls into the water, but also one that is pushed to the right.

No. 13 Pacific Dunes, Bandon, Oregon

◠

13th Hole, 444 Yards, Par 4

Scenic Holes

The ocean some seventy-five feet below on the left is an impressive sight, but so are the huge dunes and expanses of sand on the right. There happened to be a perfect amount of room in between to create an exquisite hole.

**No. 14 St. Andrews Links (Old Course),
St. Andrews, Scotland**

◠

14th Hole, 618 Yards, Par 5

Links Holes

This hole is defined by the huge Hell bunker that ends about eighty yards short of the green. You can play short of it, over it, or to the left of it, and the strategy may differ from day to day depending on the wind, the quality of your tee shot, and your state of mind.

**No. 15 Somerset Hills Country Club,
Bernardsville, New Jersey**

◠

15th Hole, 394 Yards, Par 4

Strategic Holes

The choice is whether to risk fading a driver around the dogleg, setting up a wedge approach, or laying back and leaving a longer shot to a green guarded on the front and left by a stream.

No. 16 Cypress Point Club, Pebble Beach, California

◯

16th Hole, 231 Yards, Par 3

Strategic Holes

The carry of some 200 yards over the ocean not only makes for a dazzling setting, it brings out the universal desire to be a hero. There is an option to make a shorter carry, but only by aiming well to the left of the green. Valor often wins out over discretion, because the temptation of taking on the challenge and pulling off a great shot is so strong.

No. 17 National Golf Links of America, Southampton, New York

◯

17th Hole, 375 Yards, Par 4

Exclusive Holes

This hole plays downhill to a reasonably wide fairway, so it's fair to call it a potential birdie hole. The question is which line to take off the tee. The view of the green is best from the right side, but that's where the fairway bunkers are.

No. 18 Pebble Beach Golf Links, Pebble Beach, California

◯

18th Hole, 543 Yards, Par 5

Scenic Holes

Everyone can admire the beautiful view on this hole that bends gently around the Pacific Ocean, but it plays differently for different types of players. Pros and long-hitting amateurs need to decide whether to flirt with the water on their first and second shots in an effort to get home in two, or to play it conservatively. Average players merely hope they won't uncork any wild shots that will spoil their enjoyment of the scenery.

DIRECTORY OF HOLES

UNITED STATES

Arizona
Desert Forest Golf Club, Carefree
7th hole, par 5, Strategic Holes
Desert Highlands Golf Club, Scottsdale
1st hole, par 4, Scenic Holes
**Gallery Golf Club at Dove Mountain
(North Course), Marana**
9th hole, par 5, Long Holes

California
Bel-Air Country Club, Los Angeles
11th hole, par 4, Classic Holes
Cypress Point Golf Club, Pebble Beach
15th hole, par 3, Exclusive Holes
16th hole, par 3, Strategic Holes,
Ultimate Dream 18
17th hole, par 4, Scenic Holes
**Los Angeles Country Club (North Course),
Los Angeles**
11th hole, par 3, Exclusive Holes
Olympic Club (Lake Course), San Francisco
7th hole, par 4, Short Holes
16th hole, par 5, Hard Holes
Pebble Beach Golf Links, Pebble Beach
7th hole, par 3, Short Holes
8th hole, par 4, Holes Anyone Can Play
17th hole, par 3, Historic Holes
18th hole, par 5, Scenic Holes, Ultimate Dream 18
**Pelican Hill Golf Club (North Course),
Newport Coast**
17th hole, par 5, Scenic Holes
PGA West (Stadium Course), La Quinta
6th hole, par 3, Long Holes
17th hole, par 3, Bunkerless Holes
Riviera Country Club, Pacific Palisades
10th hole, par 4, Short Holes, Ultimate Dream 18
16th hole, par 3, Well-Bunkered Holes
18th hole, par 4, Hard Holes
San Francisco Golf Club, San Francisco
7th hole, par 3, Classic Holes
SilverRock Resort, La Quinta
16th hole, par 4, Long Holes
Spyglass Hill Golf Course, Pebble Beach
4th hole, par 4, Holes Anyone Can Play,
Ultimate Dream 18
Torrey Pines Golf Course (South Course)
12th hole, par 4, Long Holes
Vintage Club (Mountain Course), Indian Wells
16th hole, par 4, Scenic Holes

Colorado
Castle Pines Golf Club, Castle Rock
10th hole, par 4, Mountain Holes
16th hole, par 3, Well-Bunkered Holes
Cherry Hills Country Club, Cherry Hills Village
1st hole, par 4, Historic Holes
The Club at Cordillera (Summit Course), Edwards
16th hole, par 3, Mountain Holes
Ironbridge Golf Club, Glenwood Springs
13th hole, par 5, Mountain Holes
Sanctuary Golf Course, Sedalia
4th hole, par 5, Mountain Holes

Connecticut
TPC River Highlands, Cromwell
15th hole, par 4, Short Holes

Florida
Bay Hill Club and Lodge, Orlando
6th hole, par 5, Water Holes
18th hole, par 4, Hard Holes
Black Diamond Ranch (Quarry Course), Lecanto
15th hole, par 4, Modern Holes

Doral Golf Resort & Spa (Blue Monster), Miami
18th hole, par 4, Water Holes
Seminole Golf Club, Juno Beach
6th hole, par 4, Exclusive Holes
TPC Sawgrass (Stadium Course), Ponte Vedra Beach
9th hole, par 5, Hard Holes
14th hole, par 4, Modern Holes
16th hole, par 5, Holes Anyone Can Play
17th hole, par 3, Water Holes
**World Woods Golf Club (Pine Barrens Course),
Brooksville**
4th hole, par 5, Short Holes

Georgia
Atlanta Athletic Club (Highlands Course), Duluth
15th hole, par 3, Water Holes
Augusta National Golf Club, Augusta
12th hole, par 3, Strategic Holes, Ultimate Dream 18
13th hole, par 5, Exclusive Holes
14th hole, par 4, Bunkerless Holes
16th hole, par 3, Historic Holes
Ocean Forest Golf Club, Sea Island
18th hole, par 4, Exclusive Holes

Hawaii
Challenge at Manele, Lanai City
12th hole, par 3, Scenic Holes
Kapalua Resort (Plantation Course), Kapalua
18th hole, par 5, Long Holes
Princeville at Hanelei (Prince Course), Princeville
15th hole, par 5, Holes Anyone Can Play

Illinois
Chicago Golf Club, Wheaton
2nd hole, par 4, Exclusive Holes
Cog Hill Golf & Country Club (No. 4 Course), Lemont
18th hole, par 4, Long Holes
Kemper Lakes Golf Club, Kildeer
17th hole, par 3, Water Holes
Medinah Country Club (No. 3 Course), Medinah
13th pole, par 3, Hard Holes
**Olympia Fields Country Club (North Course),
Olympia Fields**
14th hole, par 4, Classic Holes

Kansas
Prairie Dunes Country Club, Hutchinson
8th hole, par 4, Classic Holes,
Ultimate Dream 18

Maine
Sugarloaf Golf Club, Carabassett Valley
11th hole, par 3, Mountain Holes

Maryland
**Baltimore Country Club (Five Farms East Course),
Timonium**
6th hole, par 5, Classic Holes
Bulle Rock, Havre de Grace
13th hole, par 4, Holes Anyone Can Play
**Congressional Country Club (Blue Course),
Bethesda**
18th hole, par 4, Long Holes
Whiskey Creek Golf Club, Ijamsville
18th hole, par 5, Holes Anyone Can Play

Massachusetts
Myopia Hunt Club, South Hamilton
1st hole, par 4, Short Holes
3rd hole, par 3, Long Holes
4th hole, par 4, Historic Holes
Nantucket Golf Club, Siasconset
7th hole, par 4, Exclusive Holes
Salem Country Club, Peabody
13th hole, par 4, Classic Holes

The Country Club (Composite Course), Brookline
4th hole, par 4, Strategic Holes
17th hole, par 4, Historic Holes
TPC Boston, Norton
4th hole, par 4, Short Holes

Michigan
Arcadia Bluffs Golf Club, Arcadia
9th hole, par 3, Holes Anyone Can Play
Crystal Downs Country Club, Frankfort
5th hole, par 4, Strategic Holes
7th hole, par 4, Classic Holes
**Oakland Hills Country Club (South Course),
Bloomfield Hills**
5th hole, par 4, Historic Holes
16th hole, par 4, Water Holes
Tullymore Golf Club, Stanwood
6th hole, par 4, Well-Bunkered Holes

Minnesota
**Giants Ridge Golf & Ski Resort (Quarry Course),
Biwabik**
8th hole, par 4, Modern Holes
Hazeltine National Golf Club, Chaska
16th hole, par 4, Water Holes

Montana
Old Works Golf Club, Anaconda
6th hole, par 5, Modern Holes

Nebraska
Sand Hills Golf Club, Mullen
4th hole, par 4, Well-Bunkered Holes
7th hole, par 4, Short Holes

Nevada
Montreux Golf and Country Club, Reno
17th hole, par 4, Mountain Holes
Shadow Creek Golf Club, Las Vegas
17th hole, par 3, Modern Holes

New Jersey
Baltusrol Golf Club (Lower Course), Springfield
17th hole, par 5, Long Holes
Liberty National Golf Club, Jersey City
17th hole, par 4, Scenic Holes
Pine Valley Golf Club, Pine Valley
5th hole, par 3, Hard Holes
7th hole, par 5, Well-Bunkered Holes
13th hole, par 4, Exclusive Holes
Plainfield Country Club, Plainfield
12th hole, par 5, Water Holes
Ridgewood Country Club (Center Nine), Ridgewood
6th hole, par 4, Short Holes
Somerset Hills Country Club, Bernardsville
15th hole, par 4, Strategic Holes,
Ultimate Dream 18
Trump National Golf Club, Bedminster
6th hole, par 4, Water Holes

New Mexico
Black Mesa Golf Club, La Mesilla
16th hole, par 5, Holes Anyone Can Play

New York
Bethpage State Park (Black Course), Farmingdale
4th hole, par 5, Well-Bunkered Holes
5th hole, par 4, Strategic Holes
10th hole, par 4, Holes Anyone Can Play
15th hole, par 4, Hard Holes
Fishers Island Club, Fishers Island
4th hole, par 4, Bunkerless Holes
11th hole, par 3, Exclusive Holes
Garden City Golf Club, Garden City
14th hole, par 4, Exclusive Holes

Maidstone Club, East Hampton
9th hole, par 4, Classic Holes
National Golf Links of America, Southampton
3rd hole, par 4, Strategic Holes
17th hole, par 4, Exclusive Holes, Ultimate Dream 18
Oak Hill Country Club (East Course), Rochester
13th hole, par 5, Hard Holes
Quaker Ridge Golf Club, Scarsdale
6th hole, par 4, Classic Holes
Sebonack Golf Club, Southampton
18th hole, par 5, Scenic Holes
Shinnecock Hills Golf Club, Southampton
14th hole, par 4, Classic Holes
16th hole, par 5, Exclusive Holes
Westchester Country Club (West Course), Rye
1st hole, par 4, Short Holes
Winged Foot Golf Club (West Course), Mamaroneck
10th hole, par 3, Classic Holes
18th hole, par 4, Historic Holes

North Carolina
Pinehurst Resort and Country Club (No. 2 Course), Pinehurst
2nd hole, par 4, Classic Holes
13th hole, par 4, Holes Anyone Can Play
18th hole, par 4, Historic Holes
Pine Needles Lodge & Golf Club, Southern Pines
3rd hole, par 3, Holes Anyone Can Play
Quail Hollow Club, Charlotte
18th hole, par 4, Hard Holes
Wade Hampton Golf Club, Cashiers
18th hole, par 5, Mountain Holes

Ohio
Double Eagle Golf Club, Galena
17th hole, par 4, Exclusive Holes
Firestone Country Club (South Course), Akron
16th hole, par 5, Long Holes
Inverness Club, Toledo
7th hole, par 4, Bunkerless Holes
18th hole, par 4, Historic Holes
Muirfield Village Golf Club, Dublin
14th hole, par 4, Water Holes
Scioto Country Club, Columbus
18th hole, par 4, Historic Holes

Oklahoma
Southern Hills Country Club, Tulsa
18th hole, par 4, Hard Holes

Oregon
Bandon Dunes, Bandon Dunes
4th hole, par 4, Modern Holes
Pacific Dunes, Bandon Dunes
8th hole, par 4, Well-Bunkered Holes
11th hole, par 3, Holes Anyone Can Play
13th hole, par 4, Scenic Holes, Ultimate Dream 18
Pumpkin Ridge Golf Club (Witch Hollow Course), North Plains
14th hole, par 5, Modern Holes
Sunriver Resort (Crosswater Course), Bend
12th hole, par 5, Long Holes

Pennsylvania
Aronimink Golf Club, Newtown Square
1st hole, par 4, Classic Holes
Huntsville Golf Club, Shavertown
2nd hole, par 4, Modern Holes
Merion Golf Club (East Course), Ardmore
11th hole, par 4, Historic Holes
13th hole, par 3, Short Holes
18th hole, par 4, Long Holes
Oakmont Country Club, Oakmont
3rd hole, par 4, Well-Bunkered Holes, Ultimate Dream 18
8th hole, par 3, Long Holes
17th hole, par 4, Short Holes

Philadelphia Country Club (Spring Mill Course), Gladwyne
3rd hole, par 5, Historic Holes

Rhode Island
Newport Country Club, Newport
14th hole, par 3, Historic Holes
Wannamoisett Country Club, Rumford
3rd hole, par 3, Classic Holes

South Carolina
Harbour Town Golf Links, Hilton Head Island
17th hole, par 3, Holes Anyone Can Play
Kiawah Island Golf Resort (Ocean Course), Kiawah Island
2nd hole, par 5, Strategic Holes, Ultimate Dream 18
17th hole, par 3, Hard Holes
18th hole, par 4, Modern Holes
The Cliffs at Glassy, Landrum
13th hole, par 3, Mountain Holes

Tennessee
The Honors Course, Ooltewah
9th hole, par 4, Modern Holes

Texas
Barton Creek Resort & Spa (Fazio Foothills Course), Austin
9th hole, par 3, Holes Anyone Can Play
Colonial Country Club, Fort Worth
5th hole, par 4, Classic Holes

Vermont
Ekwanok Country Club, Manchester
7th hole, par 5, Mountain Holes
Stowe Mountain Club, Stowe
5th hole, par 4, Mountain Holes

Virginia
The Homestead (Cascades Course), Hot Springs
12th hole, par 4, Mountain Holes

Washington
Chambers Bay, University Place
2nd hole, par 4, Modern Holes
14th hole, par 4, Long Holes
TPC Snoqualmie Ridge, Snoqualmie
14th hole, par 4, Mountain Holes

Wisconsin
Blackwolf Run (River Course), Kohler
11th hole, par 5, Water Holes
Erin Hills Golf Course, Hartford
14th hole, par 5, Strategic Holes
Whistling Straits (Straits Course), Haven
11th hole, par 5, Well-Bunkered Holes
17th hole, par 3, Holes Anyone Can Play
18th hole, par 4, Hard Holes

INTERNATIONAL HOLES

Argentina
Jockey Club (Red Course), San Isidro
18th hole, par 4, Bunkerless Holes

Australia
Barnbougle Dunes, Bridport, Tasmania
4th hole, par 4, Short Holes
15th hole, par 4, Strategic Holes
Commonwealth Golf Club, South Oakleigh, Victoria
16th hole, par 4, Strategic Holes
17th hole, par 4, Australia/New Zealand Holes
Ellerston Golf Course, Ellerston, New South Wales
7th hole, par 4, Australia/New Zealand Holes
16th hole, par 4, Exclusive Holes
Kingston Heath Golf Club, Cheltenham, Victoria
3rd hole, par 4, Short Holes
6th hole, par 4, Australia/New Zealand Holes

Metropolitan Golf Club, South Oakleigh, Victoria
5th hole, par 4, Australia/New Zealand Holes
Newcastle Golf Club, Fern Bay, New South Wales
7th hole, par 3, Australia/New Zealand Holes
New South Wales Golf Club, La Perouse, New South Wales
5th hole, par 5, Australia/New Zealand Holes
6th hole, par 3, Strategic Holes
14th hole, par 4, Bunkerless Holes
Palm Meadows Golf Course, Carrara, Queensland
18th hole, par 5, Australia/New Zealand Holes
Royal Adelaide Golf Club, Seaton, South Australia
3rd hole, par 4, Bunkerless Holes
14th hole, par 4, Hard Holes
Royal Melbourne Golf Club (East Course), Black Rock, Victoria
17th hole, par 5, Well-Bunkered Holes
Royal Melbourne Golf Club (West Course), Black Rock, Victoria
6th hole, par 4, Australia/New Zealand Holes, Ultimate Dream 18
10th hole, par 4, Short Holes
17th hole, par 4, Classic Holes
The Dunes Golf Links, Rye, Victoria
17th hole, par 3, Australia/New Zealand Holes
The National Golf Club (Moonah Course), Cape Schank, Victoria
2nd hole, par 5, Australia/New Zealand Holes
The National Golf Club (Old Course), Cape Schank, Victoria
7th hole, par 3, Australia/New Zealand Holes
The Peninsula Country Golf Club (North Course), Frankston, Victoria
2nd hole, par 3, Australia/New Zealand Holes
Thirteenth Beach Golf Links (Beach Course), Barwon Heads, Victoria
13th hole, par 4, Australia/New Zealand Holes
Victoria Golf Club, Cheltenham, Victoria
9th hole, par 5, Australia/New Zealand Holes

Austria
Fontana Golf Club, Vienna
18th hole, par 5, Continental Europe Holes
Golf Eichenheim, Kitzbühel
7th hole, par 4, Mountain Holes

Bermuda
Mid Ocean Club, Tucker's Town
5th hole, par 4, Strategic Holes

Brazil
Terravista Golf Course, Trancoso
14th hole, par 3, Modern Holes

Canada
Bigwin Island Golf Club, Huntsville, Ontario
6th hole, par 4, Modern Holes
Devil's Paintbrush, Caledon Village, Ontario
13th hole, par 3, Hard Holes
Fairmont Banff Springs Golf Course, Banff, Alberta
4th hole, par 3, Scenic Holes
Fairmont Chateau Whistler Golf Club, Whistler, British Columbia
8th hole, par 3, Mountain Holes
Fairmont Jasper Park Golf Course, Jasper, Alberta
9th hole, par 3, Mountain Holes
Glen Abbey Golf Club, Oakville, Ontario
18th hole, par 5, Water Holes
Greywolf Golf Course, Panorama, British Columbia
6th hole, par 3, Scenic Holes
Highlands Links, Ingonish Beach, Nova Scotia
15th hole, par 5, Classic Holes
16th hole, par 5, Bunkerless Holes
Kananaskis Country Golf Course (Mount Kidd Course), Kananaskis Village, Alberta
16th hole, par 3, Mountain Holes
National Golf Club of Canada, Woodbridge, Ontario
7th hole, par 4, Exclusive Holes

Redtail Golf Course, Port Stanley, Ontario
6th hole, par 4, Exclusive Holes
Royal Montreal Golf Club (Blue Course), Ile Bizard, Quebec
16th hole, par 4, Water Holes
The Links at Crowbush Cove, Morell, Prince Edward Island
11th hole, par 5, Holes Anyone Can Play

China
Mission Hills Golf Club (Norman Course), Shenzhen
4th hole, par 3, Bunkerless Holes
Mission Hills Golf Club (Olazabal Course), Shenzhen
15th hole, par 5, Modern Holes

Dominican Republic
Casa de Campo (Teeth of the Dog Course), La Romana
7th hole, par 3, Scenic Holes
17th hole, par 4, Water Holes

England
Ganton Golf Club, Ganton
7th hole, par 4, Well-Bunkered Holes
Royal Ashdown Forest Golf Club (Old Course), Forest Row
11th hole, par 3, Bunkerless Holes
Royal Birkdale Golf Club, Southport
12th hole, par 3, Links Holes
Royal Liverpool Golf Club, Hoylake
1st hole, par 4, Bunkerless Holes
2nd hole, par 4, Well-Bunkered Holes
Royal Lytham & St. Annes Golf Club, Lytham St. Annes
17th hole, par 4, Well-Bunkered Holes
Royal North Devon Golf Club, Westward Ho!
6th hole, par 4, Links Holes
Royal St. George's Golf Club, Sandwich
14th hole, par 5, Links Holes
The Addington Golf Club, Croydon
12th hole, par 3, Bunkerless Holes
Wentworth Club (West Course), Virginia Water
17th hole, par 5, Bunkerless Holes
Woodhall Spa Golf Club (Hotchkin Course), Woodhall Spa
5th hole, par 3, Well-Bunkered Holes

France
Golf de La Boulie (La Vallée Course), Versailles
10th hole, par 3, Continental Europe Holes
Golf de Morfontaine, Senlis
7th hole, par 4, Exclusive Holes
Golf de Seignosse, Seignosse
17th hole, par 4, Water Holes
Golf de Sperone, Bonifacio, Corsica
13th hole, par 4, Continental Europe Holes
16th hole, par 5, Short Holes
Le Golf National (Albatross Course), Guyancourt
15th hole, par 4, Continental Europe Holes
Les Bordes, Saint Laurent-Nouan
11th hole, par 4, Continental Europe Holes

Germany
Club zur Vahr, Garlstedt
6th hole, par 5, Strategic Holes
Golf Club Gut Lärchenhof, Cologne
4th hole, par 3, Continental Europe Holes
Hamburger Golf Club, Hamburg
17th hole, par 4, Continental Europe Holes

Indonesia
Nirwana Bali Golf Club, Tabanan, Bali
7th hole, par 3, Scenic Holes, Ultimate Dream 18

Ireland
Ballybunion Golf Club (Old Course), Ballybunion
6th hole, par 4, Bunkerless Holes
11th hole, par 4, Links Holes, Ultimate Dream 18
Carne Golf Links, Belmullet
17th hole, par 4, Modern Holes

County Sligo Golf Club, Rosses Point
17th hole, par 4, Links Holes
Doonbeg Golf Club, Doonbeg
14th hole, par 3, Short Holes
9th hole, par 3, Links Holes
Enniscrone Golf Club, Enniscrone
16th hole, par 5, Bunkerless Holes
Lahinch Golf Club, Lahinch
5th hole, par 3, Links Holes
Old Head Golf Links, Kinsale
4th hole, par 4, Scenic Holes
13th hole, par 3, Long Holes
Portmarnock Golf Club, Portmarnock
14th hole, par 4, Links Holes
The European Club, Brittas Bay
13th hole, par 5, Links Holes
Tralee Golf Club, Tralee
12th hole, par 4, Hard Holes
Waterville Golf Links, Waterville
17th hole, par 3, Links Holes

Italy
Pevero Golf Club, Porto Servo
15th hole, par 5, Continental Europe Holes

Japan
Hirono Golf Club, Kobe
5th hole, par 3, Well-Bunkered Holes
Kawana Resort (Fuji Course), Ito
15th hole, par 5, Scenic Holes

Mexico
Cabo del Sol (Ocean Course), Cabo San Lucas
17th hole, par 3, Modern Holes
18th hole, par 4, Scenic Holes
Four Seasons Golf Club Punta Mita, Bahia de Banderas
hole 3B, par 3, Water Holes

Nepal
Himalayan Golf Course, Pokhara
5th hole, par 5, Mountain Holes

Netherlands
Kennemer Golf & Country Club, Zandvoort
1st hole (B Course), par 4, Continental Europe Holes
Noordwijkse Golf Club, Noordwijk
8th hole, par 4, Continental Europe Holes

New Zealand
Cape Kidnappers, Hawke's Bay
17th hole, par 4, Australia/New Zealand Holes
Gulf Harbour Country Club, Whangaparaoa
16th hole, par 4, Australia/New Zealand Holes
Kauri Cliffs, Matauri Bay
7th hole, par 3, Scenic Holes
17th hole, par 4, Australia/New Zealand Holes
Paraparaumu Beach Golf Club, Paraparaumu Beach
16th hole, par 3, Bunkerless Holes
17th hole, par 4, Australia/New Zealand Holes

Northern Ireland
Royal County Down Golf Club, Newcastle
3rd hole, par 4, Strategic Holes
9th hole, par 4, Long Holes, Ultimate Dream 18
Royal Portrush Golf Club (Dunluce Links), Portrush
5th hole, par 4, Bunkerless Holes
14th hole, par 3, Links Holes

Portugal
Praia D'El Rey Golf & Beach Resort, Obidos
4th hole, par 4, Continental Europe Holes
Penha Longa Hotel & Golf Resort (Atlantic Course), Linho
6th hole, par 5, Continental Europe Holes

San Lorenzo Golf Club, Almancil
6th hole, par 4, Continental Europe Holes

Scotland
Carnoustie Golf Links (Championship Links), Carnoustie
6th hole, par 5, Historic Holes
16th hole, par 3, Long Holes
18th hole, par 4, Hard Holes
Cruden Bay Golf Club, Cruden Bay
7th hole, par 4, Links Holes
Kingsbarns Golf Links, Kingsbarns
6th hole, par 4, Strategic Holes
15th hole, par 3, Water Holes
Loch Lomond Golf Club, Luss
5th hole, par 3, Modern Holes, Ultimate Dream 18
Machrihanish Golf Club, Campbeltown
1st hole, par 4, Links Holes, Ultimate Dream 18
Muirfield (Honourable Company of Edinburgh Golfers), Gullane
9th hole, par 5, Exclusive Holes
13th hole, par 3, Well-Bunkered Holes
17th hole, par 5, Historic Holes
18th hole, par 3, Strategic Holes
Nairn Golf Club, Nairn
5th hole, par 4, Holes Anyone Can Play
North Berwick Golf Club, North Berwick
13th hole, par 4, Links Holes
15th hole, par 3, Historic Holes
Prestwick Golf Club, Prestwick
1st hole, par 4, Historic Holes
17th hole, par 4, Links Holes
Royal Dornoch Golf Club (Championship Course), Dornoch
14th hole, par 4, Links Holes
Royal Troon Golf Club (Old Course), Troon
8th hole, par 3, Short Holes
10th hole, par 4, Bunkerless Holes
11th hole, par 4, Long Holes
St. Andrews Links (Old), St. Andrews
11th hole, par 3, Historic Holes
14th hole, par 5, Links Holes, Ultimate Dream 18
16th hole, par 4, Well-Bunkered Holes
17th hole, par 4, Hard Holes
The Gleneagles Hotel (Kings Course), Auchterarder
5th hole, par 3, Classic Holes
Turnberry Resort (Ailsa Course), Turnberry
9th hole, par 4, Links Holes
16th hole, par 4, Water Holes
Western Gailes Golf Club, Irvine
17th hole, par 4, Holes Anyone Can Play

South Africa
Durban Country Club, Durban
3rd hole, par 5, Well-Bunkered Holes
Fancourt Country Club & Golf Estate (Links Course), George
3rd hole, par 4, Hard Holes
Pinnacle Point Beach and Golf Resort, Mossel Bay
8th hole, par 4, Scenic Holes

Spain
Campo de Golf El Saler, Olivia
17th hole, par 3, Continental Europe Holes
Club de Golf Valderrama, Sotogrande
4th hole, par 5, Modern Holes
15th hole, par 3, Continental Europe Holes
Real Club de Golf Sotogrande, Sotogrande
7th hole, par 4, Continental Europe Holes

Sweden
Barsebäck Golf & Country Club (New), Malmö
17th hole, par 4, Continental Europe Holes
Falsterbo Golf Club, Falsterbo
7th hole, par 4, Continental Europe Holes

Switzerland
Golf Club Crans-sur-Sierre, Crans-sur-Sierre
7th hole, par 4, Mountain Holes

INDEX

PHOTO CREDITS

Clive Barber Photography: 128, 178 bottom right, 222 top left, 249

Aidan Bradley: 101, 114 bottom right, 181, 193, 225

Charles Briscoe-Knight: 31, 93, 127, 136–137, 174, 177, 180, 21, 264, 295 top right

Richard Castka/Sportpix International: 179, 234

Didier Chicot: 261

Courtesy Honourable Company of Edinburgh Golfers/Alastair Brown/: 45

Courtesy Black Mesa Golf Club: 60

Courtesy Desert Forest Golf Club: 135 top right

Courtesy Desert Forest Golf Club: 7

Courtesy Devil's Paintbrush Golf Course: 114 bottom left

Courtesy Doral Golf Resort & Spa at Marriott Resort: 135 bottom right

Courtesy Eichenheim Golf & Ski Resort: 190 bottom left

Courtesy El Saler Golf Club: 268

Courtesy Fontana Golf Club: 262

Courtesy Four Seasons Golf Club Punta Mita: 120–121

Courtesy Ganton Golf Club: 160 top left

Courtesy Giants Ridge Resort/ Scott Kemper/: 226

Courtesy Gut Lärchenhof Golf Club: 258

Courtesy Kohler Co.: 110, 129, 160 bottom left, 70 bottom right

Courtesy Le Golf National: 266 bottom left

Courtesy National Golf Club of Canada: 52

Courtesy of The Resort at Pelican Hill: 11

Courtesy Peninsula Country Golf Club: 273 bottom right

Courtesy Pevero Golf Club: 267

Courtesy Sanctuary Golf Course: 189

Courtesy Terravista Golf Course: 232

Courtesy TPC Boston: 78

Courtesy Tullymore Golf Club: 158

Courtesy The Vintage Club/ Jim Bartsch: 18 top left

Courtesy Whiskey Creek Golf Club: 71

Dick Durrance II: 161, 182 top left, 194, 197 bottom right, 233, 245 top right

Ron Fream/Golfplan: 187

Richard Gagnon: 247

John and Jeannine Henebry: 23 top left, 26, 27, 30 top left, 50, 55 top right, 59 top right, 81, 84, 107 bottom right, 109, 112 bottom left, 124–125, 159 top left, 162, 166, 184–185, 190 bottom right, 200, 201, 229, 293 top right

Eric Hepworth: 28, 34 top left, 176, 204, 212, 290 top left

Paul Hundley: 148

©PDI: Chris John: 242 bottom left

John R. Johnson/Golfphotos: 56–57, 88–89, 100, 223, 227, 243, 292 center left

Russell Kirk/Golf Links Photographs: 32, 33, 35, 36, 61, 65 top right, 67 bottom left, 79, 80 top left, 92, 102 bottom left, 107 bottom left, 108, 112 top left, 123 top right, 141, 156, 167, 182 bottom left, 213, 231, 235 bottom right, 236–237, 238, 245 top left, 248, 251 top left , 260, 266 bottom right, 269, 274, 275

Jim Krajicek: 49 bottom right

L.C. Lambrecht Photography: 12, 17, 24–25, 30 top right, 34 top right, 37, 38, 40–41, 42, 43, 44, 46, 49 top right, 51 bottom right, 54, 55 top left, 59 top left, 62, 67 bottom right, 75, 77, 83 bottom left, 87 top left, 87 top right, 90, 95 bottom right, 96, 98 top left, 98 top right, 99, 102 top left, 103, 113, 115, 118, 119, 122, 126 bottom left, 126 top left, 130, 131, 132 top left, 133, 134, 138, 139 bottom right, 145 bottom right, 145 top right, 146, 147, 150, 151, 154, 155 bottom right, 163, 164, 170, 173, 175, 186, 191, 195, 196, 205 top left, 207, 209, 210, 211, 215, 218, 219, 222 top right, 224 top right, 228, 230, 239, 240, 244, 251 top right, 280–281, 290 bottom left, 290 center left, 291 center right, 292 bottom left, 293 bottom right, 294 bottom left, 294 center left, 295 center right

Gary Lisbon: 2, 20, 82, 140, 142 bottom left, 172 top right, 272, 273 top right, 276 top left, 278, 279, 282, 283, 284, 286, 287, 291 bottom right

Brian Morgan Golf Photography: 10, 51 top right, 123 bottom right, 142 bottom right, 144, 183, 214, 241, 263

Mark Newcombe/Visions in Golf: 155 top right, 171, 192

Tom Pantages: 29, 80 bottom left, 91

Richard W. Rochfort: 242 top left

Wood Sabold: 19, 224 top left, 294 top left

David Scaletti: 15, 16 top right, 18 bottom left, 22, 47, 48, 76, 86, 116, 143, 149, 157, 159 top right, 165, 178 bottom left, 206, 216, 235 top right, 252–253, 254, 255, 257, 265, 270–271, 276 bottom left, 277, 285, 288–289, 292 top left

Evan Schiller: 8, 13, 14, 16 top left, 23 top right, 39 top left, 53, 58, 63, 64, 66, 68–69, 70 bottom left, 72–73, 74, 83 bottom right, 85, 94, 97, 117, 135 top right, 168–169, 198–199, 202–203, 205 top right, 217, 220–221, 246, 291 top right, 293 center right, 295 bottom right

Phil Sheldon/Golf Picture Library: 104–105, 132 bottom left, 152–153, 208, 250, 256; Liz Anthony, 39 top right, 65 bottom right; Karina Hoskyns, 259; Nic Brook, 172 top left

Watson Publishing: 106

Mark Whitright/Golfphotos: 188, 197 center

Peter Wong: 4–5, 95 top right, 111

Case: Nirwana Bali Golf Club, Tabanan, Bali, Hole #7
©David Scaletti

Editor: Margaret L. Kaplan
Designer: Jessica Shatan Heslin/Studio Shatan, Inc.
Photo Research: Cristian Pena, Laurie Platt Winfrey, Carousel Research, Inc.

Cataloging-in-Publication Data:
Barrett, David.
 Golf's dream 18s / by David Barrett.
    p. cm.
 ISBN 978-0-8109-4982-9
 1. Golf courses. I. Title. II. Title: Golf's dream eighteens.

 GV975.B35 2009
 796.352'068—dc22

                        2008055014

Please see page 303 for photograph credits.

Printed and bound in China
10 9 8 7 6 5 4 3 2 1

Abrams books are available at special discounts when purchased in quantity
for premiums and promotions as well as fundraising or educational use.
Special editions can also be created to specification. For details, contact
special markets@abramsbooks.com, or the address below.

115 West 18th Street
New York, NY 10011
www.abramsbooks.com